Innovation Station

Strategies for Success in India's Evolving Business Ecosystem

Sai Sankarsh Dasa

Copyright © 2023 by Sai Sankarsh Dasa

All rights reserved.

This book or any portion thereof may not be reproduced or used in any manner whatsoever without the express written permission of the respective writer of the respective content except for the use of brief quotations in a book review.

The writer of the respective work holds sole responsibility for the originality of the content and The Write Order is not responsible in any way whatsoever.

Printed in India

ISBN: 978-93-5776-471-1 (PB)

First Printing, 2023

The Write Order

A division of Nasadiya Technologies Private Ltd.

Koramangala, Bangalore

Karnataka-560029

THE WRITE ORDER PUBLICATIONS.

www.thewriteorder.com

Edited by Anagha Somannakoppa

Typeset by MAP Systems, Bengaluru

Book Cover designed by Malik

Publishing Consultant - Deeksha

Contents

1. **Introduction** 1
   - A brief introduction to the author
   - The purpose of the book
   - The importance of innovation and new trends in the Indian market

2. **The Landscape of Indian Markets** 13
   - Overview of India's economic growth and potential
   - Key sectors driving India's economy
   - Challenges and opportunities in the Indian market

3. **Unearthing Local Opportunities** 29
   - Identifying gaps in local markets
   - Case study: Panchami and the Pooja oil market
   - Tips for spotting untapped potential along with real-time examples

4. **AI: The Digital Revolution in Indian Businesses** 75
   - Overview of AI and its growing relevance

- The advantages and disadvantages of AI in business
- How AI can drive growth for small and medium businesses
- AI applications for automating tasks, with practical examples
- Case studies of successful AI adoption in India

5. The Power of Social Media and Digital Marketing   107
- Evolution of social media in India
- Strategies for leveraging social media platforms
- Case studies of successful social media campaigns in India

6. Innovating Marketing Strategies   139
- Traditional marketing vs. new trends
- Integrating technology into marketing efforts
- Performance marketing
- Adapting global marketing strategies to the Indian context

7. Luxury Brand Management in India   177
- Challenges and opportunities in India's luxury market
- Strategies for establishing and managing luxury brands
- Case studies of successful luxury brands in India

8. Embracing Cultural and Demographic Diversity   191
- India's cultural and demographic landscape
- Adapting products and services to cater to diverse segments
- Creating inclusive marketing campaigns

9. **Sustainability and Ethical Practices**   205
   - The importance of sustainability and ethical practices in business
   - Integrating sustainability into business operations and marketing strategies
   - Case studies of sustainable and ethical brands in India

10. **Navigating the Regulatory Environment**   215
    - Understanding India's regulatory framework
    - Compliance and legal considerations for businesses
    - Strategies for minimizing risks and maximizing opportunities

11. **Fostering Innovation and Entrepreneurship**   229
    - Encouraging a culture of innovation within organizations
    - Supporting the growth of the entrepreneurial ecosystem in India
    - Future trends and opportunities for Indian entrepreneurs

12. **Conclusion**   245
    - Key takeaways from the book
    - The importance of continuous innovation in India's evolving market
    - A call to action for entrepreneurs and business leaders

1

Introduction

About the Author

Meet Sai Sankarsh, an insightful entrepreneur and business leader who has a sharp eye for the dynamic Indian market. Sai was born into a business family in Bangalore, India, and at the age of 13, he embarked on his entrepreneurial journey by joining the family business and gaining valuable experience. This exposure ignited his passion for innovation and gave him a deep understanding of market trends.

Sai has an MBA in International Business and Luxury Brand Management from Paris, which has given him a wealth of knowledge about the global business environment. He has traveled extensively throughout the UK and Europe, which has enabled him to gain insights into international markets and consumer perspectives.

Throughout his career, Sai has always emphasized the importance of continuous innovation and adaptation to stay ahead in the competitive world of business. As a result, he has become a leading authority on social media trends, marketing innovation, and sustainable business practices for entrepreneurs and business leaders alike.

In addition to his professional pursuits, Sai is also a passionate wildlife enthusiast who advocates for nature conservation. He encourages businesses and entrepreneurs to prioritize corporate social responsibility (CSR) and giving back to nature.

Sai's book, "Innovating India: Unleashing the Power of Emerging Markets and New Trends," is a testament to his unique perspective, expertise, and passion for innovation in the rapidly growing Indian market. He aims to inspire and guide entrepreneurs and business leaders as they navigate the challenges and opportunities of the 21st century.

The purpose of the book "Innovating India: Unleashing the Power of Emerging Markets and New Trends" is to highlight the significance of innovation and value addition in the Indian market. With the rise of digital presence, businesses need to keep up with the constantly changing trends and adapt to new strategies. India, being an emerging economic powerhouse, has successfully embraced these changes and scaled its businesses to new heights.

This book is a comprehensive guide for entrepreneurs and business leaders, providing insights into various aspects of the Indian market, such as social media trends, marketing strategies, luxury brand management, and sustainability. As the Indian market continues to evolve, it is crucial for businesses to stay ahead of the curve and adapt to changing customer preferences, emerging technologies, and new market trends. Drawing from the author's personal experiences and observations of India's dynamic market transformation, this book offers practical knowledge and insights.

In the following chapters, we will explore

1. The Landscape of Indian Markets: Gain an understanding of India's economic growth, the key sectors driving its economy, and the challenges and opportunities that lie ahead.

2. Unearthing Local Opportunities: Learn how to identify gaps in local markets and discover how the author's own venture, Panchami, has capitalized on the untapped potential of the Pooja oil market.

3. The Power of Social Media and Digital Marketing: Delve into the evolution of social media in India and uncover strategies for leveraging these platforms to engage with customers and drive business growth effectively.

4. Innovating Marketing Strategies: Discover how to integrate technology into marketing efforts and adapt global marketing strategies to the unique Indian context.

5. Luxury Brand Management in India: Understand the challenges and opportunities in India's luxury market and explore strategies for establishing and managing luxury brands in the country.

6. Embracing Cultural and Demographic Diversity: Learn how to adapt products and services to cater to India's diverse cultural and demographic landscape and create inclusive marketing campaigns that resonate with a wide range of consumers.

7. Sustainability and Ethical Practices: Recognize the importance of sustainability and ethical practices in business and learn how to integrate these principles into your operations and marketing strategies.

8. Navigating the Regulatory Environment: Develop an understanding of India's regulatory framework and the compliance and legal considerations that businesses must take into account.

9. Fostering Innovation and Entrepreneurship: Discover how to encourage a culture of innovation within organizations and support the growth of the entrepreneurial ecosystem in India.

By examining these various aspects of the Indian market, this book will equip you with the knowledge and tools necessary to innovate, adapt, and thrive in the face of change. Whether you are an established business owner or an aspiring entrepreneur, "Innovating India" will inspire you to embrace the power of emerging markets and new trends and guide you on your journey toward success in the dynamic Indian market.

The Significance of Innovation and Emerging Trends in India's Market

With its booming economy and the growing number of consumers, India has become a hub for innovative ideas and new trends in the worldwide business scene. As a market that offers ample opportunities, it is crucial for businesses to remain ahead of the game and adjust to the constantly evolving dynamics of this lively and varied country. Let's dive into this chapter to understand the significance of innovation and emerging trends in the Indian market and examine the fundamental factors that fuel this progress.

Demographic Dividend and Consumer Demand

India boasts one of the youngest populations globally, with over 65% of its citizens aged below 35 years. This demographic advantage has resulted in a significant increase in consumer demand across diverse industries, including retail, e-commerce, technology, and entertainment. As this young population is more receptive to new trends and innovations, it is crucial for enterprises to adapt to their changing needs and preferences.

Technological Advancements

The Indian market has undergone a major transformation in recent years, thanks to the rapid pace of technological advancements. With the widespread adoption of the internet and smartphones, consumers have gained easy access to information, which has greatly impacted their purchase decisions and interaction with businesses. The result of this digital revolution era has been the emergence of new business models and marketing strategies, which have compelled companies to innovate in order to stay competitive.

The impact of technology has been felt across all sectors of the economy, from retail to manufacturing to healthcare. For instance, e-commerce has become a popular mode of shopping, with a growing number of consumers opting for online purchases. This has led to the rise of digital marketplaces, which offer a wide variety of products and services to consumers at competitive prices.

Moreover, the use of mobile apps has transformed the way businesses engage with their customers. Companies now use mobile apps to offer personalized and targeted marketing to their customers, which has resulted in higher customer engagement and loyalty.

In conclusion, the digital revolution era has brought about significant changes to the Indian market, and businesses that are able to innovate and keep up with the latest trends are better positioned to succeed in today's competitive landscape.

Government Initiatives and Support

The Indian government has been instrumental in promoting innovation and entrepreneurship in the country. With initiatives such as 'Make in India,' 'Digital India,' and 'Startup India,' the government has created a conducive environment for businesses to thrive.

The 'Make in India' initiative, in particular, has played a vital role in boosting local manufacturing and promoting self-reliance. The program aims to encourage both domestic and foreign companies to manufacture their products in India, thereby boosting economic growth, creating employment opportunities, and reducing dependence on imports.

Similarly, 'Digital India' has been a game-changer in the country's digital transformation journey. The program aims to provide digital infrastructure and connectivity to every citizen, enabling them to access government services, education, healthcare, and other essential services online. This has not only improved access to services but also created new opportunities for businesses to leverage digital technologies to reach a wider audience.

The 'Startup India' initiative has been a boon for the country's startup ecosystem. The program provides funding, mentorship, and other resources to startups, helping them to scale up and compete globally. This has led to the emergence of many successful startups in India, particularly in the technology and e-commerce sectors.

Overall, the Indian government's efforts to promote innovation and entrepreneurship have had a significant impact on the country's business ecosystem. These initiatives have not only created new opportunities for businesses but also helped to drive economic growth and create employment opportunities for millions of people.

Globalization and Market Integration

With the Indian market's increasing integration into the global economy, local businesses are now exposed to new ideas, trends, and best practices from around the world. This heightened exposure has resulted in greater competition, and as a result, Indian companies must continually innovate and distinguish themselves in the market.

The Rise of the Middle Class

The rapid growth of India's middle class has been a major contributing factor in the country's overall development. With rising incomes and greater access to information, this consumer base is becoming increasingly demanding when it comes to the products and services they consume. The days of the "one-size-fits-all" approach are long gone, and businesses are now expected to offer more personalized and unique experiences that cater to the specific needs and preferences of their customers.

As a result, companies are investing heavily in research and development to keep up with the latest trends and innovations. The focus is on creating products and services that not only meet the basic needs of the consumer but also provide added value and a sense of exclusivity. This is particularly true in the hospitality and tourism industry, where customers are looking for unique and memorable experiences that go beyond the standard offerings.

In addition, there is a growing demand for eco-friendly and sustainable products and services as consumers become more conscious of their impact on the environment. Businesses are responding to this trend by adopting green practices and incorporating eco-friendly materials and processes into their operations.

Overall, the changing consumption patterns and preferences of India's middle class present both challenges and opportunities for businesses. Those that are able to stay ahead of the curve and provide innovative, personalized, and sustainable solutions will likely see continued success in the years to come.

The Evolution of the Startup Ecosystem

Over the last decade, the Indian startup ecosystem has witnessed exponential growth, making it one of the most vibrant and dynamic markets globally. With a plethora of success stories emerging in various sectors, including e-commerce, fintech, healthcare, and education, the Indian startup ecosystem has created a culture of innovation and collaboration that inspires businesses of all sizes to adopt new technologies and practices to stay competitive.

In recent years, the Indian market has witnessed a surge in startups in emerging sectors such as agritech, edtech, healthtech, and cleantech, driven by the need to address the challenges of the country's vast population and diverse demographics. The Indian startup ecosystem has also gained significant traction from global investors, with billions of dollars in funding pouring into the market, making India one of the most attractive destinations for startups.

The Indian government has been instrumental in fostering the growth of the startup ecosystem by launching various initiatives and programs, such as Startup India and Digital India, aimed at promoting innovation, entrepreneurship, and digital transformation. These initiatives have not only provided startups with access to funding, mentorship, and networking opportunities but have also encouraged the adoption of new technologies, making India a hub for innovation.

Moreover, the COVID-19 pandemic has accelerated the adoption of digital technologies, enabling startups to leverage digital platforms to reach customers and scale their businesses. The pandemic has also highlighted the importance of innovation and technology in addressing the challenges of the new normal, such as remote work, online education, and healthcare.

In conclusion, the Indian startup ecosystem has come a long way, and its growth trajectory shows no signs of slowing down. With a supportive government, a diverse and growing market, and a culture of innovation, India is poised to become a global leader in the startup space. The future looks bright for Indian startups, and we can expect to see more success stories emerge in the years to come.

A. E-commerce and Digital Payments

E-commerce has revolutionized the way consumers shop and businesses sell in India. The convenience of online shopping, coupled with affordable smartphones and growing internet penetration, has led to a surge in the number of online shoppers. Innovations such as personalized product recommendations, augmented reality, and conversational commerce are further enhancing the customer experience and driving growth in the sector.

Digital payments have also witnessed significant growth, driven by government initiatives and the increasing adoption of smartphones. From mobile wallets and UPI to contactless payments and cryptocurrencies, the Indian market is embracing new payment technologies and moving towards a cashless economy.

B. Artificial Intelligence and Machine Learning

Artificial intelligence (AI) and machine learning (ML) have emerged as powerful tools for businesses to enhance their operations, customer engagement, and decision-making. From chatbots and virtual assistants to predictive analytics and automation, AI and ML are enabling businesses to optimize their processes, reduce costs, and deliver more personalized experiences to customers.

In India, several sectors, including healthcare, agriculture, manufacturing, and finance, are increasingly incorporating AI and ML technologies to drive growth and improve efficiency. The adoption of these advanced technologies has opened up new avenues for innovation and is shaping the future of the Indian market.

C. Sustainable and Eco-friendly Products and Practices

Growing environmental concerns and increasing awareness of the impact of businesses on the planet have led to a greater focus on sustainability and eco-friendly practices in India. Consumers are becoming more conscious of their choices and are seeking out products and services that align with their values.

In response, businesses are embracing eco-friendly practices, such as using renewable energy sources, reducing waste, and adopting circular economy models. Innovations in sustainable materials, packaging, and production processes are also gaining traction as companies strive to minimize their environmental footprint and cater to the demands of environmentally-conscious consumers.

D. Personalization and Customization

In today's market, customers are increasingly seeking personalized experiences, prompting businesses to use data and technology to meet these demands. Customized clothing, personalized nutrition plans, and curated travel experiences are just a few examples of how personalization is becoming a crucial factor in the Indian market. With the help of big data analytics, AI, and ML, businesses can gain valuable insights into customer preferences and behaviors. This enables them to create tailor-made products and services that cater to each customer's unique needs and desires.

E. The Gig Economy and Remote Work

In India, the gig economy has become increasingly popular due to the rise of digital platforms and the demand for on-demand services.

This type of economy consists of temporary, freelance, or flexible jobs and has spurred the development of innovative business models and platforms connecting gig workers with potential clients. Popular examples include ride-sharing services, food delivery apps, and freelance marketplaces. The COVID-19 pandemic has further accelerated the trend towards remote work, resulting in the development of new tools and technologies that facilitate remote collaboration and communication, as well as new strategies for managing remote teams and maintaining productivity.

F. Health and Wellness

India's health and wellness industry has experienced remarkable growth due to the increasing awareness of health and well-being among consumers. This has resulted in a surge in demand for innovative products and services, including fitness apps, wearable technology, telemedicine, and personalized health coaching.

Moreover, businesses in India are recognizing the significance of mental health and well-being. As a result, companies are offering employee wellness programs and online mental health services to meet this growing need.

To succeed in the ever-changing Indian market, entrepreneurs and business leaders must remain flexible, embrace change, and continuously innovate their products, services, and strategies. By doing so, they can take advantage of the vast opportunities in the Indian market and establish a strong foundation for long-term success.

2

The Landscape of Indian Markets

Overview of India's Economic Growth and Potential

India, the world's largest democracy and the seventh-largest country by land area, has experienced significant economic growth and development over the past few decades. In this subsection, we will provide an overview of India's economic growth and potential, as well as the driving forces behind its ascent as a global economic powerhouse.

1. Historical Perspective

After gaining independence, India implemented a socialist-based economic model that prioritized self-reliance and a planned economy. However, this approach only resulted in limited growth and hindered the country's ability to compete internationally. In 1991, India had to confront a severe economic crisis, which prompted a series of economic reforms that liberalized the economy, opened up markets to foreign investment, and supported private sector development.

These reforms marked a significant shift in India's economic direction, leading to accelerated growth, increased foreign investments, and the emergence of a burgeoning middle class ever since India has consistently been ranked among the fastest-growing major economies globally.

2. Economic Growth and Development

Since the 1991 reforms, India's economy has experienced remarkable growth, with its Gross Domestic Product (GDP) surging from $266 billion to over $2.6 trillion in 2020. Although the COVID-19 pandemic has temporarily slowed down this growth, India's long-term economic prospects appear optimistic, with predictions of a vigorous recovery and sustained expansion in the years to come.

A few critical factors have driven India's economic growth, including:

- A sizable and growing population, which has resulted in a vast labor force and a substantial consumer market.

- A shift from an agriculture-based economy to a more diversified one, with the burgeoning of the services and manufacturing sectors.

- A burgeoning middle class with increasing disposable incomes and changing consumption habits.

- Greater foreign investment, as global businesses, recognize India's potential for growth and favorable demographics.

- Government policies and initiatives that support economic growth attract foreign investment and encourage entrepreneurship.

3. Key Sectors Driving Growth

India's economic growth has been propelled by the strong performance of several key sectors, which include:

- Services: The services sector, which encompasses industries such as IT, telecommunications, retail, and tourism, has been the primary driver of India's economic growth, accounting for over 55% of its GDP. India's IT and business process outsourcing (BPO) industries, in particular, have become global leaders, generating significant foreign exchange earnings and employment opportunities.

- Manufacturing: The manufacturing sector has also played a crucial role in India's economic development. The 'Make in India' initiative, launched in 2014, aims to transform India into a global manufacturing hub by encouraging domestic and foreign investment in the sector. Key industries within the manufacturing sector include automotive, pharmaceuticals, textiles, and electronics.

- Agriculture: Agriculture remains an essential part of India's economy, employing nearly 42% of the country's workforce. While the sector's share of GDP has declined over the years, it still plays a critical role in ensuring food security, providing raw materials for other industries, and supporting rural livelihoods.

- Infrastructure and Construction: As India continues to urbanize and modernize, the infrastructure and construction sectors have emerged as significant contributors to economic growth. Investments in transportation, energy, and urban development projects have generated employment opportunities and facilitated the country's overall development.

4. Challenges and Opportunities

Despite its impressive growth and development, India faces several challenges that need to be addressed to sustain and accelerate its economic progress. These challenges include:

- Infrastructure deficits: India's infrastructure, such as roads, ports, and power generation facilities, lags behind that of other major economies, hampering growth and development.

- Skill development and education: India's young and growing population presents both an opportunity and a challenge. To harness the full potential of this demographic dividend, India needs to invest in skill development and education, ensuring that its workforce is equipped to compete in the global market.

- Income inequality and poverty: Despite its economic growth, India continues to grapple with high levels of income inequality and poverty. Ensuring that the benefits of growth are distributed more equitably among the population is crucial for the country's long-term development.

- Environmental sustainability: Rapid industrialization and urbanization have led to growing concerns about environmental degradation and resource depletion. India needs to adopt more sustainable growth models and prioritize environmental conservation to ensure long-term prosperity.

- <u>Ease of doing business:</u> While India has made significant strides in improving its business environment, further reforms are needed to streamline regulations, reduce red tape, and create a more conducive environment for entrepreneurship and investment.

Despite these challenges, India's economic potential remains immense. With its vast consumer market, favorable demographics, and growing appetite for innovation, the country presents a wealth of opportunities for businesses, investors, and entrepreneurs. Key areas for future growth and innovation include:

- <u>Technology and innovation:</u> India's tech sector has already demonstrated its global competitiveness. Continued investment in R&D and the development of cutting-edge technologies, such as artificial intelligence, machine learning, and advanced manufacturing, will drive growth in this sector and position India as a leader in the global innovation landscape.

- <u>Renewable energy:</u> As the world shifts toward cleaner and more sustainable energy sources, India's renewable energy sector presents significant growth potential. Investments in solar, wind, and other renewable technologies will not only drive economic growth but also contribute to the country's energy security and help address environmental concerns.

- <u>Healthcare and biotechnology:</u> With a growing demand for healthcare services and an aging population, India's healthcare sector offers immense opportunities for growth and innovation. Investments in biotechnology, pharmaceuticals, and medical devices can help India meet its healthcare needs and become a global leader in these industries.

- E-commerce and digital services: India's rapidly growing internet penetration and smartphone adoption present significant opportunities for e-commerce and digital services providers. As more consumers embrace online shopping and digital payments, businesses that can innovate and adapt to this changing landscape will thrive.

In conclusion, India's economic growth and potential are underpinned by a combination of demographic, technological, and policy factors. While challenges remain, the country's diverse and dynamic market offers a wealth of opportunities for businesses and entrepreneurs to innovate and grow. By addressing its challenges and capitalizing on its strengths, India is well-positioned to continue its ascent as a global economic powerhouse and a hub for innovation and development.

Key Sectors Driving India's Economy

India's rapid economic growth can be attributed to the impressive performance of several key sectors. These sectors, which include services, manufacturing, agriculture, and infrastructure, have contributed to the country's development and have shaped its economic landscape. In this section, we will delve deeper into these key sectors, as well as discuss India's imports, exports, and service sectors that are driving its economy.

1. Services Sector

India's economy is primarily supported by the services sector, which accounts for over 55% of the Gross Domestic Product (GDP).

This sector encompasses various industries, such as Information Technology (IT), Business Process Outsourcing (BPO), retail, tourism, telecommunications, and financial services. The IT and BPO industries, in particular, have emerged as global leaders, generating substantial foreign exchange earnings and creating employment opportunities for millions. The success of technology giants like Infosys, Wipro, and Tata Consultancy Services (TCS) showcases India's expertise in IT services, with technology hubs sprouting in cities like Bangalore, Hyderabad, and Pune.

Telecommunications is another thriving segment of the services sector. India stands as the world's second-largest market for mobile phone subscribers, and the growth of e-commerce, digital payments, and other digital services in the country is fueled by affordable smartphones and widespread internet access.

The retail and tourism industries have experienced significant growth, driven by India's expanding middle class. More people now travel within and outside the country for leisure and business purposes. The financial services sector has also witnessed remarkable progress, bolstered by the expansion of banking and non-banking financial institutions. Additionally, the increasing penetration of insurance products and mutual funds has contributed to this growth.

2. Manufacturing Sector

The manufacturing sector has played a crucial role in driving India's economic growth, contributing approximately 14-16% to its GDP. Key industries in this sector include automotive, pharmaceuticals, textiles, and electronics.

In 2014, the 'Make in India' initiative was launched to promote the manufacturing industry and position India as a global manufacturing hub. This initiative has been successful in attracting both domestic and foreign investments, particularly in the automotive and electronics sectors. As a result, numerous international companies have established manufacturing facilities in India.

India is also a major player in the pharmaceutical industry, ranking third globally in terms of volume and 13th in terms of value. The country supplies over 50% of the global demand for vaccines and 40% of the generic drug demand in the United States, making it a significant exporter of generic drugs.

3. Agriculture Sector

India's economy heavily relies on agriculture, which employs approximately 42% of the workforce and contributes 16-18% to the country's GDP. Although the sector's share of GDP is decreasing, it remains crucial for ensuring food security, supporting rural livelihoods, and providing raw materials for other industries. India is a significant producer of food grains, fruits, vegetables, spices, and pulses, and it also exports agricultural products such as tea, rice, wheat, and cotton. However, the sector faces several challenges, including the impacts of climate change, inadequate infrastructure, and low productivity, which need to be addressed to unlock its full potential.

4. Infrastructure and Construction Sector

India's economic growth is experiencing significant boosts from the infrastructure and construction sectors as the country urbanizes and modernizes. The development of transportation, energy, and urban infrastructure has created job opportunities and facilitated overall progress. To enhance the country's infrastructure and promote port-led industrialization, the government has launched ambitious initiatives such as the 'Smart Cities Mission' and the 'Sagarmala Programme.' Moreover, investments in renewable energy, highways, and railways are expected further to drive growth in these sectors in the years ahead.

5. Imports and Exports

India's economy has immensely benefited from international trade, with a diverse export basket that encompasses traditional items like textiles, gems and jewelry, and agricultural products, as well as high-value goods such as pharmaceuticals, automobiles, and IT services. In 2020, India's total merchandise exports reached approximately $313 billion, with the United States, United Arab Emirates, China, and European countries serving as the major export destinations. India's skilled labor force, cost advantages, and robust manufacturing base in key sectors contribute to its export competitiveness.

On the import side, India depends on imports of critical goods such as crude oil, gold, and electronic components. In 2020, India's total merchandise imports reached approximately $467 billion, with China, the United States, the United Arab Emirates, and Saudi Arabia serving as the primary import partners. The country's imports are driven by the increasing demand for energy, capital goods, and raw materials to support its expanding economy.

6. Service Exports

India has made remarkable progress in the export of services, in addition to merchandise exports. This progress is primarily attributed to the IT and BPO industries, which accounted for over 45% of the total service exports in 2020. Other notable service exports include financial services, travel, and transportation. The demand for IT and BPO services in developed countries has significantly contributed to the rapid growth of India's service exports over the past two decades. One of India's competitive advantages in this area is its vast pool of skilled professionals, English-speaking workforce, and cost-effectiveness compared to developed countries.

In summary, India's economic growth is largely driven by the exceptional performance of the services, manufacturing, agriculture, and infrastructure sectors. Its diverse export basket and growing role as a service exporter have also made significant contributions to its economic development. Continued investment in these sectors and addressing the challenges they face will enable India to sustain its growth trajectory and further enhance its position as a global economic powerhouse.

Challenges and Opportunities in the Indian Market

The Indian economy boasts rapid growth and vast potential, providing a multitude of opportunities for businesses and investors. Nevertheless, the market poses various challenges that require attention to achieve sustainable growth and development. This section will explore the significant challenges and opportunities present in the Indian market.

Challenges

1. Infrastructure Deficits

One of the primary challenges facing the Indian market is its inadequate infrastructure. The country's roads, ports, railways, and power generation facilities lag behind those of other major economies, hindering growth and development. Insufficient and unreliable power supply, for instance, has a detrimental impact on the manufacturing, services, and agriculture sectors, resulting in reduced efficiency and productivity.

2. Skill Development and Education

India's young and expanding population presents both an opportunity and a challenge. To harness the full potential of this demographic dividend, India needs to invest in skill development and education, ensuring that its workforce is equipped to compete in the global market. However, a significant portion of India's youth remains unskilled or under-skilled, resulting in a mismatch between industry demands and the available workforce.

3. Income Inequality and Poverty

Despite its impressive economic growth, India continues to grapple with high levels of income inequality and poverty. According to the World Bank, in 2019, approximately 22% of India's population lived below the national poverty line. Ensuring that the benefits of growth are distributed more equitably among the population is crucial for the country's long-term development and social stability.

4. Environmental Sustainability

Rapid industrialization and urbanization have raised concerns about environmental degradation and resource depletion. India ranks among the world's largest emitters of greenhouse gases, and air pollution remains a significant issue in many of its cities. To secure long-term prosperity, the country must embrace more sustainable growth models and prioritize environmental conservation.

5. Ease of Doing Business

While India has made significant strides in improving its business environment, further reforms are required to streamline regulations, reduce red tape, and create a more conducive environment for entrepreneurship and investment. Bureaucratic hurdles, corruption, and complex tax structures can deter potential investors and impede the growth of businesses in the country.

Opportunities

1. Demographic Dividend

India's young and growing population provides a substantial labor force and a significant consumer market. With a median age of around 28 years, India stands as one of the youngest nations worldwide. This demographic dividend offers opportunities for businesses in diverse sectors, including consumer goods, education, healthcare, and financial services. The demand for these products and services is anticipated to grow in line with the population, presenting favorable conditions for market expansion.

2. Technological Innovation

India has emerged as a global hub for technology and innovation, particularly in the IT and startup sectors. With a large pool of skilled professionals and a strong entrepreneurial culture, India possesses the potential to take a leading role in cutting-edge technologies such as artificial intelligence, machine learning, and advanced manufacturing. This presents opportunities for businesses to innovate and leverage India's thriving technology ecosystem.

3. Renewable Energy

As the world transitions towards cleaner and more sustainable energy sources, India's renewable energy sector holds immense growth potential. The country has established ambitious targets for renewable energy capacity, aiming to reach 450 gigawatts by 2030. Investments in solar, wind, and other renewable technologies will not only spur economic growth but also enhance the country's energy security and address environmental concerns.

4. E-commerce and Digital Services

India's rapidly expanding internet penetration and increasing smartphone adoption offer significant opportunities for e-commerce and digital service providers. With more consumers embracing online shopping and digital payments, businesses that can innovate and adapt to this evolving landscape are poised to thrive. The e-commerce market in India is projected to experience exponential growth in the coming years, providing immense potential for both domestic and international players.

5. Infrastructure Development

The government's emphasis on infrastructure development presents numerous opportunities for businesses in the construction, transportation, and energy sectors. Ambitious initiatives such as the 'Smart Cities Mission,' 'Sagarmala Programme,' and 'Bharatmala Pariyojana' aim to revolutionize India's infrastructure landscape. Companies that engage in these projects and contribute to the country's infrastructure growth have the potential to reap significant benefits.

6. Healthcare and Biotechnology

With a rising demand for healthcare services and an aging population, India's healthcare sector presents immense opportunities for growth and innovation. Investments in biotechnology, pharmaceuticals, and medical devices can aid India in meeting its healthcare requirements and positioning itself as a global leader in these industries. The country's pharmaceutical industry, in particular, has exhibited significant promise, establishing India as a major exporter of generic drugs.

7. Rural Markets

India's rural markets offer untapped potential for businesses across various sectors, considering that over 65% of the country's population resides in rural areas. As infrastructure improves and rural incomes rise, there is anticipated growth in demand for consumer goods, financial services, and other products in these regions. Companies that can customize their offerings to meet the unique needs and preferences of rural consumers can capitalize on this potential for growth.

8. Manufacturing and 'Make in India'

The 'Make in India' initiative provides opportunities for businesses to establish manufacturing facilities in the country and tap into the vast domestic market. As the government strives for increased self-reliance and aims to reduce imports, companies that can localize production and leverage India's cost advantages will gain a competitive edge in the market.

In conclusion, the Indian market presents a unique blend of challenges and opportunities. While addressing infrastructure deficits, skill development, and environmental sustainability is crucial, the country's demographic dividend, technological innovation, and potential in sectors such as renewable energy, e-commerce, and healthcare offer tremendous growth potential. Businesses that can navigate these challenges and seize the opportunities presented by India's market are poised for success in this rapidly expanding economy.

3

Unearthing Local Opportunities

Identifying Gaps in Local Markets

India's dynamic and diverse market presents a wealth of local opportunities for businesses and entrepreneurs. By identifying gaps in local markets, companies can innovate and introduce products and services that cater to unmet needs and create value for consumers. In this subsection, we will explore how businesses can identify gaps in local markets and leverage innovation to capitalize on these opportunities.

1. Market Research and Analysis

Identifying gaps in local markets requires businesses to conduct thorough market research and analysis. By understanding the unique characteristics, consumer preferences, and competitors' strengths and weaknesses of the local market, businesses can determine areas of unmet demand for specific products or services. Market research can be conducted using surveys, focus groups, and analyzing secondary data sources such as industry reports and market studies. Additionally, businesses should consider demographic, geographic, and cultural factors that may impact consumer behavior in local markets.

IKEA is an excellent example of a company that successfully penetrated the Indian market through extensive research and analysis. The Swedish furniture and home furnishings retailer is renowned for its affordable and stylish products that cater to a wide range of customers. Before entering the Indian market, IKEA conducted thorough market research and analysis to understand the unique preferences, needs, and challenges of the Indian consumer.

IKEA's research revealed that the Indian market was characterized by diverse preferences, cultural influences, and economic factors. To cater to this market's specific needs, IKEA made several adjustments to its offerings and approach.

1. Product Adaptation: IKEA tailored its product range to suit Indian consumers' preferences and living spaces. They introduced products designed specifically for Indian households, such as kitchenware adapted for Indian cooking, foldable furniture to save space, and colorful textiles that resonate with Indian design sensibilities.

2. Localization of Supply Chain: To keep prices affordable, IKEA established a robust local supply chain by sourcing materials and partnering with local manufacturers. This helped the company reduce costs and ensure that its products were competitively priced in the Indian market.

3. Store Format: Realizing that Indian consumers prefer a more personalized shopping experience, IKEA redesigned its store format in India to include room sets inspired by local homes, live demonstrations, and interactive workshops.

4. Digital Presence: To cater to India's growing online consumer base, IKEA launched a robust e-commerce platform and mobile app to provide a seamless shopping experience for customers. The company also leveraged social media platforms to engage with customers and create brand awareness.

5. Payment Options: IKEA adapted its payment options to cater to the Indian market's preferences, offering cash-on-delivery, digital wallets, and other popular payment methods to make transactions convenient and hassle-free for customers.

6. After-Sales Services: Understanding that Indian consumers value after-sales support, IKEA introduced services like home delivery, assembly support, and extended warranties to enhance customer satisfaction.

7. Sustainability and Social Initiatives: IKEA emphasized its commitment to sustainability and social responsibility in India, engaging in initiatives like partnering with local NGOs, supporting women's empowerment, and investing in renewable energy.

These targeted strategies helped IKEA successfully penetrate the Indian market and resonate with Indian consumers. The company's thorough market research and analysis allowed it to adapt and tailor its offerings to meet the unique needs and preferences of the

Indian market, which contributed to its success. As a result, IKEA has witnessed a positive response from Indian consumers, and its stores continue to attract large crowds, reflecting the effectiveness of its market research and the appeal of its adapted products and services.

2. Identifying Consumer Pain Points

To succeed in the market, businesses must understand the pain points of their target audience. They can achieve this by directly communicating with customers through interviews or focus groups or indirectly by monitoring customer feedback and online reviews. By identifying consumer challenges, businesses can develop innovative solutions that set them apart from competitors. For instance, if customers in a specific market face persistent power outages, a company may introduce solar-powered appliances or energy storage solutions to alleviate the issue.

A great example of a company that succeeded in the Indian market by identifying consumer pain points is OYO Rooms. Founded in 2013 by Ritesh Agarwal, OYO Rooms is a hotel aggregator and booking platform that provides budget hotels with standardized services, ensuring a hassle-free and affordable accommodation experience for travelers.

1. Identifying the Pain Points: Agarwal recognized that the Indian budget hotel industry was highly fragmented, lacking standardization and transparency in pricing, quality, and services. This made it difficult for travelers to find reliable and affordable accommodations, leading to dissatisfaction and frustration.

2. Standardizing Accommodations: To address this issue, OYO Rooms partnered with small and independent hotels, helping them to upgrade their infrastructure, services, and amenities to meet OYO's quality standards. In return, these hotels became part of the OYO network and were listed on the platform.

3. Transparent Pricing: OYO Rooms introduced transparent pricing, ensuring that customers knew the exact cost of their stay without any hidden charges. This approach helped build trust among consumers, who could make informed decisions while booking accommodations.

4. User-Friendly Booking Platform: OYO Rooms developed a user-friendly website and mobile app, enabling customers to search for, compare easily, and book hotels across various locations in India. This convenient booking process addressed the pain point of cumbersome hotel reservations, making it simpler for travelers to find suitable accommodations.

5. Customer Support: OYO Rooms also invested in providing excellent customer support. They set up a dedicated 24/7 customer care service to handle customer inquiries, complaints, and concerns. This move further addressed the pain points of travelers who often faced difficulties in communicating with hotel staff and resolving issues during their stay.

6. Expansion and Growth: The success of OYO Rooms in identifying and addressing consumer pain points led to rapid growth and expansion. The company quickly expanded its presence across India and later ventured into international markets such as

China, Malaysia, Nepal, the United Arab Emirates, and the United Kingdom.

7. Continuous Improvement: OYO Rooms has consistently worked on enhancing its offerings by introducing new services and features, such as OYO Home (offering homestays), OYO Townhouse (mid-segment hotels), and OYO Workspaces (co-working spaces). These innovations have helped the company cater to the evolving needs of Indian consumers and tap into new market segments.

The story of OYO Rooms is an excellent example of how a company can penetrate the Indian market by identifying consumer pain points and providing innovative solutions to address them. By focusing on understanding the needs of travelers and delivering standardized, affordable, and transparent accommodations, OYO Rooms has emerged as a leading player in the Indian hospitality industry.

3. Observing Global Trends and Localizing Them

One way for businesses to discover new opportunities is to keep an eye on global trends and find ways to tailor them to local markets. By observing successful products, services, or business models in other regions, companies can develop localized versions that cater to the unique needs and preferences of the local population. For example, Ola in India adapted the ride-hailing concept popularized by Uber and Lyft in Western markets to suit India's transportation landscape, while Flipkart was created based on the success of e-commerce giants like Amazon and Alibaba, specifically catering to the Indian market.

One prominent example of a company penetrating the Indian market by observing global trends and localizing them is the success story of Zomato, a food delivery and restaurant discovery platform.

1. Identifying the Global Trend: The online food ordering and delivery industry was witnessing a significant boom worldwide, with platforms like Grubhub, Just Eat, and Deliveroo gaining immense popularity in their respective markets. Zomato's founders identified this global trend and saw potential in bringing a similar service to India.

2. Localizing the Concept: Zomato started as a restaurant discovery platform in 2008, providing detailed information about restaurants, menus, and user-generated reviews. This addressed the need for organized and easily accessible information about dining options in India.

3. Expanding the Service: In 2015, Zomato entered the food delivery market, competing with existing players like Swiggy and Foodpanda. To cater to local preferences, Zomato ensured a wide variety of food options from local restaurants and popular chains, along with exclusive delivery tie-ups with popular restaurants.

4. Customizing the Experience: Zomato understood the importance of regional tastes and preferences, so it provided a platform that could be easily customized based on the user's location, language, and food preferences. They also introduced features like food recommendations, cashless payments, and discounts tailored to the Indian market.

5. Building Trust with Consumers: To address concerns related to food quality and safety, Zomato launched initiatives like Zomato Gold (a subscription-based service offering exclusive deals), Hygiene Ratings for partner restaurants (for maintaining transparency on cleanliness and food safety), and Zomato Kitchen (a cloud kitchen model that enabled restaurants to expand their reach without the overhead costs of a physical location).

6. Leveraging Local Partnerships: Zomato formed strategic partnerships with local payment providers, banks, and mobile wallets to facilitate seamless transactions. They also partnered with local delivery companies to ensure efficient delivery services in different regions.

7. Adapting to Changing Market Dynamics: Zomato has been quick to adapt to changing market dynamics, such as the rise in demand for contactless deliveries and heightened safety concerns during the COVID-19 pandemic. They introduced features like contactless delivery, temperature checks for delivery personnel, and safety badges for partner restaurants.

8. Addressing Social Causes: Zomato took the initiative to address social causes relevant to the Indian market. They launched programs like Zomato Feeding India (a food rescue organization that redistributes surplus food to the needy) and Zomato Treats (a subscription service that helps in feeding underprivileged children).

The success of Zomato in India can be attributed to its ability to observe global trends and localize them to suit the Indian market's unique needs and preferences. By understanding the pulse of the market and addressing consumer pain points, Zomato has managed to become a leading food delivery and restaurant discovery platform in India, with a presence in over 500 cities and a growing international footprint.

4. Leveraging Technology and Innovation

To address gaps in local markets, businesses must embrace technology and innovation. By exploring emerging technologies and innovative business models, they can develop solutions that cater to unmet needs. A prime example of this is the healthcare sector in India, where telemedicine has emerged as a promising solution to bridge the gap between urban and rural healthcare access. Through technology and innovative service delivery models, telemedicine platforms such as Practo and 1mg have provided quality healthcare services to previously underserved communities.

A prime illustration of a company utilizing technology and innovation to expand its reach in the Indian market is Ola Cabs. Established in 2010 by Bhavish Aggarwal and Ankit Bhati, Ola transformed the taxi and transportation industry in India by introducing a technology-oriented, on-demand ride-hailing platform. Ola's success can be attributed to various factors, such as:

1. Addressing a Real Problem: Ola recognized the challenges faced by commuters in India due to the lack of reliable and affordable taxi services. They aimed to provide a convenient and cost-effective solution by connecting passengers with drivers through a mobile app.

2. User-Friendly Interface: Ola's mobile app offers a user-friendly interface that makes booking rides simple and convenient. With features like real-time tracking, cashless payments, and in-app customer support, Ola managed to attract millions of users.

3. Technological Innovation: Ola used technology to streamline operations, improve efficiency, and enhance the user experience. They employed GPS technology to optimize route planning, machine learning algorithms for demand prediction, and data analytics to monitor driver performance and customer feedback.

4. Customized Offerings: Ola adapted its services to cater to the diverse needs of the Indian market. They introduced various car categories, such as Ola Micro, Ola Mini, Ola Prime, and Ola Lux, to suit different customer preferences and price points. They also launched Ola Auto, Ola Bike, and Ola Share to cater to users seeking more affordable and eco-friendly transportation options.

5. Expansion into Tier 2 and Tier 3 Cities: Ola identified the untapped potential in smaller cities and expanded its services to cover more than 250 cities across India, providing affordable and accessible transportation options to millions of people.

6. Local Partnerships: Ola collaborated with local car manufacturers, dealers, and financial institutions to create a robust ecosystem that supported their growth. These partnerships enabled Ola to scale its fleet rapidly and offer attractive incentives to drivers.

7. Continuous Innovation: Ola has consistently focused on innovation to stay ahead of the competition. They introduced Ola Play, an in-cab entertainment system; Ola Pass, a subscription-based service

for discounted rides; and Ola Money, a digital wallet for seamless payments.

Ola's success in the Indian market demonstrates how leveraging technology and innovation can help companies identify gaps in local markets and create value for consumers. By addressing consumer pain points and constantly evolving its offerings, Ola has become one of the largest ride-hailing platforms in India, with a presence in over 250 cities and a growing international footprint.

5. Collaborating with Local Stakeholders

Working with local stakeholders can be beneficial for businesses to spot gaps in the market and devise innovative solutions that cater to the needs of the local community. Collaborating with government agencies, non-governmental organizations, and local communities can offer valuable insights into market dynamics and help businesses understand the unique challenges and opportunities in local markets. Such partnerships can also encourage creativity by bringing together diverse perspectives and expertise. For instance, collaborating with local artisans or craftsmen can help businesses create one-of-a-kind, locally-inspired products that appeal to local tastes and preferences.

IKEA, the renowned Swedish furniture company, is a great example of a business that achieved success in the Indian market by collaborating with local stakeholders. In 2018, IKEA entered the Indian market with a long-term, localized strategy to establish a strong foothold in the furniture and home furnishings sector. The company implemented the following tactics:

1. Local Sourcing and Manufacturing: IKEA set a goal to source at least 30% of its raw materials locally to meet the Indian government's foreign direct investment (FDI) requirements. The company collaborated with local suppliers, artisans, and manufacturers to source materials like textiles, wood, and bamboo, fostering a mutually beneficial relationship with local businesses.

2. Customizing Products: IKEA adapted its product range to cater to Indian consumers' needs and preferences. They conducted extensive research into local lifestyles, traditions, and habits and introduced products like smaller furniture for compact spaces, spice boxes, pressure cookers, and rice cookers, which resonated with the Indian audience.

3. Collaborating with Local Designers: IKEA partnered with local designers and artisans to create India-specific collections that showcased traditional craftsmanship and aesthetics. These collaborations helped IKEA tap into India's rich design heritage and appeal to a wider customer base.

4. Skill Development and Training: IKEA established a Skill Development Center in India to train local workers in various aspects of retail, customer service, and furniture assembly. This initiative not only helped IKEA build a skilled workforce but also contributed to local employment and skill development. Engaging with

5. Local Communities: IKEA undertook various corporate social responsibility (CSR) initiatives in India, focusing on women's empowerment, education, and healthcare. The company

partnered with non-governmental organizations (NGOs) and local communities to create a positive impact on society.

6. Building a Sustainable Supply Chain: IKEA is committed to sourcing sustainable and renewable materials for its products and worked with local suppliers to improve their sustainability practices. The company also promoted sustainable living by offering eco-friendly products and solutions to Indian consumers.

Through these strategic collaborations with local stakeholders, IKEA managed to create a strong foothold in the Indian market. By understanding the local context, adapting its products, and working closely with local partners, IKEA demonstrated how global companies can successfully penetrate emerging markets like India while contributing to the local economy and society.

6. Experimenting with New Business Models

Exploring new business models is a great way for companies to discover untapped potential in local markets. This can involve introducing fresh distribution channels, providing personalized products or services, or implementing unique pricing strategies that cater to the specific needs of the market.

For instance, India's vast rural market has led to the development of innovative business models like micro-franchising and rural distribution networks that enable companies to reach customers in remote areas. Additionally, the success of sachet packaging in India's FMCG sector showcases how innovative pricing and packaging strategies can make products more accessible and affordable for low-income consumers.

To take advantage of India's diverse and dynamic market, businesses need to identify gaps in the local markets. To do this, they must conduct thorough market research, understand consumer pain points, observe global trends, leverage technology and innovation, collaborate with local stakeholders, and experiment with new business models. This approach can create significant opportunities for businesses in India.

Innovation is key to bridging market gaps and creating value for consumers. By fostering a culture of innovation and continuously seeking new ways to meet unmet needs, companies can differentiate themselves from competitors and gain a competitive advantage in the market. As the Indian market continues to grow and evolve, businesses that can adapt to the changing landscape and capitalize on local opportunities will be well-positioned for success.

One company that successfully penetrated the Indian market by experimenting with new business models is Byju's, an Indian educational technology (edtech) startup. Byju's leveraged technology to provide personalized learning experiences for students through their learning app, which offers engaging content, interactive quizzes, and in-depth analysis. Another example is Zomato, an Indian food delivery and restaurant aggregator startup that disrupted the traditional food delivery market in India by introducing online food ordering and delivery services. Both companies have demonstrated how experimenting with new business models and leveraging technology can create opportunities for startups to penetrate the Indian market and achieve significant growth.

Case Study: Panchami And The Pooja Oil Market

I. Introduction

    A. Background On Aromatherapy And Alternative Medicine

    B. The Importance Of Mental Health Awareness

    C. The Significance Of The Panchami Case Study

II. The Beginning: Personal Struggles Inspire A New Business Venture

    A. The Founder's Experiences With Depression And Anxiety

    B. The Discovery Of Essential Oils And Their Benefits

    C. The Connection To Hindu Lamp Lighting Rituals

III. Combining Tradition With Aromatherapy: The Panchami Product Line

    A. The Concept Of Pancha Deepam And Its Significance

    B. The Five Fragrances And Their Unique Benefits

    C. The Development Of Complementary Products, Such As Incense Sticks

IV. Challenges In Product Development And Market Entry

    A. The High Cost Of Essential Oils And Blending Difficulties

    B. The Search For The Perfect Blend And Product Pricing

    C. The Introduction Of Gst And Its Impact On Product Pricing

V. Expanding Distribution And Adoption Through Modern Trade Outlets

    A. The Pull Marketing Strategy For Retailers And Wholesalers

    B. The Role Of Existing Supply Chain Connections

    C. Success In Securing Placements In Prominent Outlets

VI. Consumer Adoption And Feedback

    A. The Importance Of Consumer Awareness And Education

    B. The Role Of Packaging And Product Presentation

    C. Positive Feedback And Testimonials From Users

VII. Lessons Learned And Best Practices

    A. The Importance Of Perseverance And Innovation

    B. The Value Of Market Research And Understanding Customer Needs

    C. The Role Of Marketing Strategies In Overcoming Challenges

VIII. Future Prospects And Growth Opportunities

    A. Potential For Product Line Expansion

    B. Opportunities For International Expansion

    C. The Role Of Technology And E-Commerce In Furthering Growth

IX. Conclusion

    A. Recap Of Panchami ☐'s Journey And Accomplishments

    B. The Significance Of The Case Study For The Aromatherapy And Alternative Medicine Industries

    C. Final Thoughts On The Future Prospects Of Panchami ☐

Introduction

The Allure of Aromatherapy and Alternative Medicine

Aromatherapy, a practice with roots tracing back thousands of years, harnesses the power of natural essential oils to improve physical and emotional well-being. By utilizing the aromatic compounds found in plants, aromatherapy offers a non-invasive and holistic approach to health and wellness, providing a natural alternative to conventional treatments. Today, as the global interest in alternative medicine continues to grow, the use of essential oils for therapeutic purposes has gained widespread recognition.

Historically, aromatherapy has played an essential role in various cultures and civilizations, from ancient Egypt to China and India. The therapeutic properties of essential oils have been explored extensively in traditional medicine systems, such as Ayurveda and traditional Chinese medicine. These ancient practices often passed down through generations, have laid the foundation for modern aromatherapy and continue to inspire contemporary practitioners.

In recent years, there has been a resurgence of interest in alternative medicine, driven by a growing awareness of the potential adverse effects of conventional treatments, an increasing desire for natural remedies, and a greater understanding of the connection between physical and mental health. As a result, the demand for essential oils has skyrocketed, leading to the emergence of numerous brands and products catering to various needs, preferences, and therapeutic objectives.

Aromatherapy can be applied in several ways, including inhalation, topical application, and even ingestion, depending on the specific oil and its intended use. The benefits of essential oils range from alleviating stress and anxiety to reducing inflammation and promoting relaxation. Some popular essential oils, such as lavender, rose, and jasmine, are renowned for their calming and uplifting properties, while others, like eucalyptus and peppermint, are known for their invigorating effects.

The growing popularity of aromatherapy has also led to increased scientific research on the therapeutic properties of essential oils. Numerous studies have demonstrated the efficacy of various oils in addressing specific ailments, such as lavender oil for sleep disturbances and anxiety or tea tree oil for combating infections. The growing body of evidence has further legitimized the use of essential oils in modern healthcare settings and contributed to the acceptance of aromatherapy as a viable complementary therapy.

Despite the numerous benefits of aromatherapy, it is essential to recognize that not all essential oils are created equal. The quality of an oil depends on factors such as the cultivation and harvesting of the plant material, the extraction method used, and the purity of the final product. Synthetic fragrances and adulterated oils, which may contain harmful chemicals, can undermine the therapeutic benefits of aromatherapy and even pose potential health risks. Therefore, it is crucial for consumers and practitioners to prioritize the use of pure, high-quality essential oils sourced from reputable suppliers.

The Importance of Mental Health Awareness

In recent years, mental health awareness has gained significant attention worldwide, and rightfully so. As society becomes increasingly more fast-paced and demanding, it is vital to prioritize mental well-being alongside physical health. Mental health awareness is essential for several reasons, including reducing stigma, encouraging early intervention, promoting overall well-being, and fostering a supportive community.

Reducing stigma: Mental health issues have long been associated with shame, fear, and misunderstanding. This stigma can prevent people from seeking help, sharing their experiences, or even acknowledging that they are struggling. By raising awareness about mental health, we can challenge misconceptions and create an environment where individuals feel more comfortable discussing their mental health concerns without fear of being judged or dismissed.

Encouraging early intervention: Mental health issues can affect anyone, regardless of age, gender, or background. Recognizing the signs of mental health problems early can make a significant difference in a person's recovery journey. When people are educated about mental health, they are more likely to seek help early on, increasing the likelihood of successful treatment and reducing the risk of long-term consequences.

Promoting overall well-being: Mental health is an integral part of overall wellness. A healthy mind and a healthy body are interconnected, and maintaining a balance between the two is crucial for well-being. By increasing awareness of mental health, we can emphasize the importance of self-care, stress management, and coping strategies that contribute to a more balanced and fulfilling life.

Fostering a supportive community: Raising mental health awareness can help create more empathetic and supportive communities where people feel comfortable sharing their experiences and seeking help. When individuals understand the importance of mental health, they are more likely to offer support and encouragement to friends, family members, or colleagues who may be struggling. This sense of community can make it easier for those affected by mental health issues to access resources, find solace, and ultimately heal.

Enhancing mental health services: Increased awareness about mental health issues can also lead to improvements in mental health care services. As more people recognize the importance of mental health, there is a greater likelihood that funding and resources will be allocated toward mental health research, treatment, and support services. This can result in more accessible, effective, and affordable mental health care for everyone.

The Significance of the Panchami Case Study

The Panchami case study is significant for several reasons, as it highlights the power of innovation, the importance of mental health, and the potential for businesses to make a meaningful impact on people's lives. This case study demonstrates how an entrepreneur can identify an unmet need and create a unique, culturally-relevant product that addresses both mental and spiritual well-being.

Innovation in traditional practices: Panchami illustrates the potential to innovate within a traditional cultural context. By combining the ancient practice of lighting lamps with modern aromatherapy, the founder created a product that appeals to a wide audience while staying true to its roots. This demonstrates the power of innovation in bridging the gap between tradition and modernity and the potential for businesses to tap into cultural practices to create unique, meaningful offerings.

Addressing mental health: Panchami's case study underscores the importance of addressing mental health in today's fast-paced, high-pressure world. By incorporating essential oils known for their mental health benefits, the company not only offers a spiritual product but also provides a natural, holistic solution for those seeking relief from stress, anxiety, and other mental health concerns. This highlights the potential for businesses to have a positive impact on people's well-being and the value of promoting mental health through innovative products.

Supporting local industries and sustainability: Panchami's commitment to using locally-sourced, ethically-produced oils and supporting the Prime Minister's Make in India project demonstrates a strong dedication to sustainability and the local industry. By prioritizing domestic production and ethical sourcing, Panchami sets an example for other businesses looking to make a positive impact on their communities and the environment.

Overcoming challenges and adapting to the market: The Panchami case study shows how perseverance, adaptability, and strategic thinking can help businesses overcome challenges and thrive in a competitive market. From dealing with taxation issues to adjusting product offerings and packaging to meet consumer preferences, Panchami's journey offers valuable lessons for entrepreneurs and businesses looking to succeed in today's rapidly-changing landscape.

Promoting awareness and education: By offering a product that combines spiritual and mental health benefits, Panchami plays a role in promoting awareness and education about mental health, alternative medicine, and the significance of traditional practices. This serves as an example for other businesses looking to create products that not only meet a market need but also contribute to a larger conversation about well-being, culture, and personal growth.

The Beginning: Personal Struggles Inspire a New Business Venture - The Founder's Experiences with Depression and Anxiety

It was during a difficult period in the founder's life that the idea for Panchami was born. Having recently moved back to India from the UK, the founder found themselves struggling with severe depression and anxiety. Adjusting to the environment in India proved to be a challenge, and they were in search of a solution to help them cope with their mental health issues.

Around this time, the founder became aware of a growing conversation about mental health in India, with many people seeking alternative treatments instead of traditional medications. This newfound openness towards mental health created a market segment ripe for exploration.

During their search for relief, the founder came across the concept of aromatherapy and decided to give it a try. They ordered a small 15mL bottle of lavender essential oil for a steep price, and upon receiving it, they were amazed by the positive effects it had on their mental state. The calming scent emitted by their bedside diffuser helped them sleep more easily and made them feel more at peace than they had in weeks.

Being a second-generation entrepreneur with a background in the oil refining business, the founder recognized the potential of essential oils in India. They saw an opportunity to merge the practice of lighting lamps, a deeply ingrained part of Hindu culture, with the benefits of aromatherapy to create a unique product that could potentially help hundreds of thousands of people.

With their personal experience as a driving force, the founder embarked on a journey to develop a range of lamp oils and incense sticks that would not only cater to the spiritual needs of Indian consumers but also provide mental health benefits. Drawing from the concept of Pancha Deepam, the founder created a line of products using five ethically and naturally sourced oils combined with essential oils known for their mental health benefits.

The founder's personal struggles with depression and anxiety served as the inspiration behind Panchami, demonstrating the power of adversity in driving innovation and giving rise to a product that has the potential to impact countless lives positively. By combining their own experiences with their knowledge of the oil market and the needs of Indian consumers, the founder transformed their struggles into a unique business venture that promotes mental well-being and spiritual growth.

The Discovery of Essential Oils and Their Benefits

Essential oils have been used for thousands of years for their aromatic and therapeutic properties. Extracted from various parts of plants, including flowers, leaves, bark, roots, and seeds, these natural compounds have been revered for their ability to promote emotional and physical well-being. Their use can be traced back to ancient civilizations such as Egypt, China, and India, where they were employed for medicinal, cosmetic, and spiritual purposes.

The process of extracting essential oils typically involves steam distillation, although other methods like cold pressing and solvent extraction are also utilized. The end result is a highly concentrated, fragrant substance that captures the essence of the plant from which it was derived.

Essential oils offer a wide range of benefits, with each oil having unique properties and applications. For example, lavender oil is known for its calming and relaxing effects, making it an excellent aid for those suffering from stress, anxiety, and insomnia. Meanwhile, eucalyptus oil has potent antimicrobial and anti-inflammatory properties that can be beneficial for respiratory issues and muscle pain relief.

In recent years, the use of essential oils has gained popularity in the field of aromatherapy – a holistic healing practice that uses natural plant extracts to improve mental, emotional, and physical well-being.

Aromatherapy harnesses the power of essential oils through various methods, such as inhalation, topical application, and diffusion. When inhaled or absorbed through the skin, these oils are believed to interact with the body's limbic system, which plays a role in regulating emotions, memory, and various physiological functions.

The benefits of essential oils are not limited to aromatherapy, however. They are also used in cosmetics, personal care products, household cleaning solutions, and even as natural flavorings and fragrances in food and beverages. As more people become aware of the potential benefits of essential oils and seek natural alternatives to synthetic chemicals, their popularity continues to grow.

In conclusion, the discovery of essential oils and their myriad benefits has led to their widespread use in various aspects of daily life. As research into their potential applications continues to expand, essential oils will likely play an even more significant role in promoting overall well-being and improving the quality of life for individuals around the world.

The Connection to Hindu Lamp Lighting Rituals

In Hinduism, lighting lamps, also known as "deep" or "diya," is an integral part of religious and spiritual practices. This ritual has deep symbolic significance and plays a crucial role in various ceremonies, festivals, and daily worship. The act of lighting a lamp signifies the triumph of light over darkness, knowledge over ignorance, and good over evil. It is believed that the presence of a lit lamp invites divine blessings, dispels negativity, and fosters an environment of peace, prosperity, and spiritual enlightenment.

Traditionally, lamps used in Hindu rituals are made from clay, brass, or other metals and are fueled by ghee (clarified butter) or vegetable oils. These oils are often chosen for their auspicious properties or specific benefits. In some cases, a blend of oils is used to create what is known as "Pancha Deepam" oil, which is a combination of five different oils, each offering unique spiritual and physical benefits.

The concept of using essential oils in the context of Hindu lamp lighting rituals is an innovative and holistic approach to incorporating the benefits of aromatherapy into traditional practices. By infusing the lamp oil with essential oils, practitioners can enjoy the therapeutic properties of these natural compounds while also adhering to the symbolic and spiritual significance of the ritual.

Essential oils such as lavender, rose, jasmine, sandalwood, and lemongrass can be used to enhance the overall experience of lamp lighting, offering a range of benefits that align with the core principles of Hinduism. For instance, lavender oil promotes relaxation and stress relief, while rose oil has the ability to uplift the mood and combat depression. Jasmine oil is believed to promote mental clarity and focus, whereas sandalwood oil is revered for its grounding and balancing properties. Lemongrass oil, on the other hand, can act as a natural air freshener, creating a clean and invigorating atmosphere.

Incorporating essential oils into the Hindu lamp-lighting ritual is a testament to the versatility and adaptability of traditional practices, as well as the growing awareness of the benefits of alternative medicine and natural remedies. By merging these two elements, practitioners can enhance the experience of this age-old ritual, embracing the healing powers of essential oils while honoring the rich symbolism and spiritual significance of lighting lamps in Hinduism.

Combining Tradition with Aromatherapy: The Panchami Product Line

The Concept of Pancha Deepam and Its Significance

The Panchami product line is a unique and innovative approach to combining the ancient tradition of Pancha Deepam with the therapeutic benefits of aromatherapy. Pancha Deepam, which translates to "five lamps" in Sanskrit, refers to the practice of using a blend of five different oils in a lamp to create an auspicious and spiritually uplifting atmosphere. This blend is believed to bring good health, wealth, knowledge, and prosperity into one's home.

The Panchami product line takes this age-old practice to new heights by incorporating essential oils into the Pancha Deepam blend, offering a range of therapeutic benefits that align with the spiritual significance of the ritual. Each product in the Panchami line is designed to promote mental health and well-being while adhering to the traditional principles of Hindu lamp lighting.

The Panchami product line includes five distinct blends, each catering to different needs and preferences. These blends are Lush Lavender, British Rose, Lemongrass, Real Jasmine, and Mystic Sandal. Each blend is carefully crafted using ethically and naturally sourced domestic oils, supporting the Make in India initiative.

Lush Lavender offers the calming benefits of lavender essential oil, helping users achieve deeper sleep and combat insomnia.

British Rose, on the other hand, is formulated to fight depression and reduce mood swings in women during menstruation. Real Jasmine is designed to manage feelings of stress and anxiety while improving concentration. Mystic Sandal aids in achieving mental clarity and revitalizing the senses, while Lemongrass serves as a popular room freshener, keeping the environment clean and invigorated.

In addition to lamp oils, the Panchami product line also includes incense sticks that complement the oil blends, offering a complete aromatic experience for users.

By merging the traditional practice of Pancha Deepam with the therapeutic benefits of essential oils, the Panchami product line offers a unique and holistic approach to self-care, mental health, and spiritual well-being. This innovative product line serves as a testament to the adaptability of ancient traditions and the growing awareness of the benefits of alternative medicine and natural remedies.

The Five Fragrances and Their Unique Benefits

Each of the five fragrances in the Panchami product line has been carefully formulated to provide unique therapeutic benefits, catering to various needs and preferences. Here's a closer look at the benefits of each fragrance:

Lush Lavender: Lavender essential oil is well-known for its calming properties, making it an ideal choice for promoting relaxation and restful sleep. Lush Lavender helps users combat insomnia and achieve deeper sleep while creating a serene atmosphere. The calming scent of lavender also helps to soothe anxiety and stress, making it a popular choice for mental well-being.

British Rose: The uplifting fragrance of British Rose is designed to combat depression and elevate mood. It has a gentle, soothing effect on emotions, making it particularly beneficial for women experiencing mood swings during menstruation. The beautiful scent of roses also creates a warm and inviting atmosphere, contributing to a sense of well-being and happiness.

Lemongrass: Lemongrass is known for its refreshing and invigorating scent, which makes it a popular choice for room freshening and revitalizing the senses. The crisp, citrusy aroma of lemongrass helps to cleanse the air and create a positive atmosphere, making it an ideal choice for those looking to energize their environment and promote mental clarity.

Real Jasmine: The exotic scent of real jasmine is designed to manage feelings of stress and anxiety while improving concentration. Known for its calming and balancing effects on emotions, jasmine essential oil helps to create a sense of inner peace and harmony. This makes Real Jasmine an excellent choice for those seeking to reduce stress levels and improve focus.

Mystic Sandal: Mystic Sandal combines the grounding and meditative properties of sandalwood essential oil to promote mental clarity and spiritual awareness. The warm, woody scent of sandalwood is known to help still the mind and deepen meditation, making Mystic Sandal an excellent choice for those looking to enhance their spiritual practice and cultivate inner tranquility.

By offering a range of fragrances that cater to different needs and preferences, the Panchami product line ensures that users can find the perfect blend to support their mental health, well-being, and spiritual growth.

The Development of Complementary Products: Incense Sticks

Understanding the need to provide a complete aromatherapy experience to its customers, Panchami expanded its product line by introducing complementary items, such as incense sticks. By offering a variety of incense sticks that complement their existing fragrances, Panchami aims to enhance the overall sensory experience and provide a more immersive atmosphere for users.

Incense sticks have long been a staple in religious and spiritual practices across various cultures, and they are especially popular in Hindu rituals. By introducing incense sticks that match the fragrances of their lamp oils, Panchami offers users the opportunity to create a cohesive environment that is both spiritually and mentally uplifting.

The incense sticks developed by Panchami share the same fragrances as the lamp oils, including Lush Lavender, British Rose, Lemongrass, Real Jasmine, and Mystic Sandal. This allows users to mix and match products based on their preferences or even layer scents to create a unique ambiance in their space.

By offering incense sticks alongside their lamp oils, Panchami acknowledges the importance of providing users with a holistic approach to aromatherapy and spiritual practice. Customers can now create a synergistic environment that promotes mental well-being, relaxation, and spiritual growth by using Panchami's products in combination. This not only enhances the user experience but also helps to solidify Panchami's position as a comprehensive provider of aromatherapy and spiritual wellness products.

Challenges in Product Development and Market Entry: The High Cost of Essential Oils and Blending Difficulties

During the development of her product, Panchami encountered a significant obstacle in the form of the high cost of essential oils. Obtaining essential oils through steam and water distillation of natural sources like flowers and plants can be significantly more expensive than synthetic fragrances. This made it challenging to strike a balance between the right blend of essential oils with the base oils while keeping costs feasible.

For instance, producing 500ml of pure jasmine oil requires at least 100 kgs of jasmine flowers, significantly impacting the final cost of the product. Panchami's goal was to offer high-quality products at an affordable price, but the costly essential oils made it difficult to achieve this balance.

To overcome this issue, Panchami worked tirelessly to experiment with various blends and ratios of essential oils and base oils to create the perfect product. They also had to search for multiple vendors and online channels to source the best quality oils at reasonable prices. Their aim was to provide a premium product without compromising on quality while making it accessible to a broader audience.

One of the challenges encountered during the market entry phase was competition from other brands that offered single oil-based products at a lower tax rate. According to the Goods and Services Tax (GST) laws in India, blending two or more edible oils without an AGMARK certification would result in a higher tax rate of 12% compared to the 5% GST rate that applies to single edible oils. As a result, Panchami's products would automatically be priced higher than their competitors.

To overcome this challenge, Panchami implemented a pull marketing strategy, focusing on retailers and wholesalers rather than consumers directly. By placing their products in well-known retail chains and online platforms, they generated awareness and demand, which eventually led to the acquisition of more retailers and wholesalers, thereby reducing their cost per acquisition. This innovative approach helped Panchami overcome the challenges posed by the high cost of essential oils and the complexities of blending, enabling them to establish a strong foothold in the market.

Expanding Distribution and Adoption through Modern Trade Outlets: The Pull Marketing Strategy for Retailers and Wholesalers

Panchami chose to implement a pull marketing approach to expand its distribution and increase product adoption. Instead of targeting consumers directly, they aimed to create awareness and demand for their products through modern trade outlets, such as renowned retail chains like DMart, Metro Cash and Carry, Big Basket, and various quick commerce portals. By doing so, they were able to establish credibility, build product visibility, and make it easier for the brand to penetrate the market.

When retailers and wholesalers saw Panchami products on the shelves of these big-name stores, they perceived the brand as a popular and fast-moving product. This perception encouraged them to stock Panchami products in their own shops, which ultimately led to increased product adoption for the brand. Panchami effectively established a strong brand presence by utilizing a pull marketing strategy. This involved leveraging the power of established retail chains and online platforms, resulting in a reduced cost per acquisition for retailers and wholesalers.

By being present in modern trade outlets, Panchami generated organic interest and demand for their products without having to offer consumer discounts or wholesaler schemes. By aligning the interests of customers, retailers, and wholesalers, Panchami successfully expanded its distribution network and increased product adoption. Ultimately, the pull marketing strategy for retailers and wholesalers proved to be a cost-effective and efficient method for Panchami to reach a wider audience and establish its place in the market.

The Role of Existing Supply Chain Connections

Leveraging existing supply chain connections played a crucial role in Panchami's market entry and growth. The founder's father had an established business in oil refining, which provided a solid foundation for the new venture. With a well-developed supply chain already in place, Panchami could seamlessly integrate its products into the existing distribution network, reducing the time and resources needed to build a new supply chain from scratch.

This advantage allowed Panchami to focus on product development and marketing efforts rather than worrying about the logistics of distribution. The existing connections with wholesalers and retailers also made it easier for Panchami to introduce its products to the market, as the brand could capitalize on the trust and relationships already established by the founder's father.

Moreover, the knowledge and expertise gained from the family's oil refining business provided valuable insights into the oil market and consumer behavior. This understanding proved to be essential in crafting a product that resonated with the target audience and met their needs.

By utilizing existing supply chain connections and building on the foundation laid by the founder's father, Panchami could quickly penetrate the market, gain credibility, and create a demand for its innovative product line. The brand's ability to tap into these resources played a significant role in its success and growth, making it a prime example of the importance of leveraging existing networks and expertise in a new business venture.

Success in Securing Placements in Prominent Outlets

Panchami's innovative approach to combining tradition with aromatherapy and mental health benefits caught the attention of prominent retail outlets. By targeting modern trade outlets such as Dmart, Metro Cash and Carry, Big Basket, and other quick commerce portals, Panchami was able to place its products alongside well-known brands, thereby increasing its visibility and credibility.

Securing placements in these prestigious outlets was essential to Panchami's success, as it not only exposed the brand to a wider audience but also helped establish a positive product positioning. Consumers were more likely to consider Panchami's offerings as high-quality and desirable due to their presence in these esteemed retail environments.

Furthermore, the brand's visibility in modern trade outlets had a ripple effect on its acceptance by smaller retailers and wholesalers. When these smaller businesses observed Panchami's products on the shelves of large, successful retailers, they were more inclined to stock the brand in their own shops, expecting it to be a fast-moving product.

This success in securing placements in prominent outlets had a significant impact on Panchami's growth, as it enabled the brand to reach a broader audience and gain the trust of both consumers and retailers. By strategically targeting modern trade outlets and capitalizing on their influence, Panchami managed to establish a strong foothold in the market, paving the way for its continued success.

Success in Securing Placements in Prominent Outlets

Panchami's innovative approach to combining tradition with aromatherapy and mental health benefits caught the attention of prominent retail outlets. By targeting modern trade outlets such as Dmart, Metro Cash and Carry, Big Basket, and other quick commerce portals, Panchami was able to place its products alongside well-known brands, thereby increasing its visibility and credibility.

Securing placements in these prestigious outlets was essential to Panchami's success, as it not only exposed the brand to a wider audience but also helped establish a positive product positioning. Consumers were more likely to consider Panchami's offerings as high-quality and desirable due to their presence in these esteemed retail environments.

Furthermore, the brand's visibility in modern trade outlets had a ripple effect on its acceptance by smaller retailers and wholesalers. When these smaller businesses observed Panchami's products on the shelves of large, successful retailers, they were more inclined to stock the brand in their own shops, expecting it to be a fast-moving product.

This success in securing placements in prominent outlets had a significant impact on Panchami's growth, as it enabled the brand to reach a broader audience and gain the trust of both consumers and retailers. By strategically targeting modern trade outlets and capitalizing on their influence, Panchami managed to establish a strong foothold in the market, paving the way for its continued success.

Consumer Adoption and Feedback

A. The importance of consumer awareness and education

When launching a new product, especially one that introduces a novel concept, consumer awareness and education become crucial factors in its success. For Panchami, a brand that combines Hindu lamp lighting rituals with aromatherapy, it was essential to educate potential customers about the benefits of essential oils and their integration into traditional practices.

The Indian market, with its diverse consumer base, presented a unique challenge for Panchami. Although the country has a rich history of Ayurvedic medicine and alternative therapies, the concept of essential oils for mental health was relatively new. Therefore, Panchami had to create awareness about the benefits of essential oils in improving mental well-being and how their product could seamlessly integrate with traditional Hindu rituals.

To achieve this, the brand leveraged various marketing channels, such as social media, blogs, and influencers, to educate the audience about the importance of mental health and the therapeutic effects of essential oils. By providing valuable information and engaging content, Panchami was able to create interest among potential customers and encourage them to try their products.

B. The role of packaging and product presentation

In addition to consumer education, the packaging and presentation of a product play a significant role in its success. Attractive and well-designed packaging can capture the attention of potential customers, convey the product's value proposition, and create a positive first impression.

For Panchami, the packaging and presentation were particularly important, as they needed to convey the essence of the brand - the fusion of traditional Hindu rituals with modern aromatherapy. The company chose to use glass packaging for its premium product line to create a sense of luxury and quality. The design elements, colors, and typography used in the packaging helped communicate the brand's identity, making it stand out on the shelves and online platforms.

Moreover, the packaging also had to cater to the needs of different market segments. Panchami introduced a more affordable, daily-use product line with plastic bottles and flexible films to appeal to a wider audience. By offering a variety of packaging options, the brand was able to cater to diverse customer preferences and price points, increasing its market penetration.

C. Positive feedback and testimonials from users

In today's digital era, consumer feedback and testimonials play a crucial role in driving brand reputation and consumer adoption. Positive reviews, testimonials, and word-of-mouth marketing can significantly impact a brand's credibility, leading to increased sales and market share.

For Panchami, the feedback from their customers was invaluable in validating the product's effectiveness and helping to refine their offerings. As users experienced the benefits of Panchami's essential oils in their daily lives, they shared their stories and positive experiences with others, creating a snowball effect of organic growth.

To leverage this positive feedback, Panchami actively encouraged customers to share their experiences on social media platforms and e-commerce websites. The brand also collaborated with influencers and bloggers who resonated with Panchami's values, creating authentic content that showcased the product's benefits.

As a result, Panchami was able to build a strong community of loyal customers who not only continued to purchase their products but also became brand advocates, spreading the word about Panchami's unique offerings.

In conclusion, Panchami's success can be attributed to its focus on consumer awareness, education, attractive packaging, and leveraging positive feedback from users. By understanding the unique challenges of the Indian market and tailoring its strategy accordingly, the brand was able to create a niche for itself in the competitive essential oils industry.

Future Prospects and Growth Opportunities

A. Potential for product line expansion

Panchami aims to diversify its offerings by expanding into other items within the pooja product line. The company's primary focus will be on integrating aromatherapy into these new products whenever possible. In cases where aromatherapy cannot be included, Panchami will emphasize high quality to ensure an upgraded and uplifting pooja experience for its customers. The expanded product line will comprise daily pooja essentials that cater to a variety of spiritual practices and preferences.

B. Opportunities for international expansion

Panchami has already initiated its international expansion by utilizing Amazon Global Shipping. The company's focus will now shift towards increasing its presence in major cities worldwide. Panchami also aims to enter Indian grocery stores in foreign markets, which will allow it to cater to the specific needs and preferences of Indian expatriates and others who share an interest in Hindu rituals and practices. By targeting these niche markets, Panchami can carve out a unique space for itself in the international arena and broaden its customer base.

C. The role of technology and e-commerce in furthering growth

Panchami's e-commerce website currently processes approximately 1,000 orders per month. In addition, the brand has a strong presence on Jio Mart, with over 4,000 orders per month. The company recognizes the need to improve its performance on other popular e-commerce platforms, such as Amazon and Flipkart, to increase its online sales further and reach a wider audience.

Technology and e-commerce are vital to Panchami's continued growth and success. By optimizing its digital presence across various platforms and utilizing data-driven marketing strategies, Panchami can ensure that it remains competitive in the rapidly evolving online marketplace.

Recap of Panchami's journey and accomplishments

Panchami's journey began with the founder's personal struggles with depression and anxiety and their discovery of the benefits of essential oils. Recognizing the potential of combining the therapeutic aspects of aromatherapy with the spiritual significance of Hindu lamp-lighting rituals, Panchami developed a unique product line of lamp oils and incense sticks. The brand has successfully overcome various product development and market entry challenges, leveraging existing supply chain connections and securing prominent retail placements.

The Panchami case study is a testament to the power of innovation in the aromatherapy and alternative medicine industries. By thoughtfully combining traditional practices with modern wellness trends, Panchami has created a niche market for itself, demonstrating that there is ample opportunity for growth and diversification in these industries. The brand's success also highlights the importance of consumer education and awareness in driving market adoption, as well as the role of e-commerce and technology in scaling the business.

Final thoughts on the future prospects of Panchami

With its unique offerings and a solid foundation in both the spiritual and wellness markets, Panchami has a promising future. The brand's plans for product line expansion, international growth, and a stronger focus on e-commerce will undoubtedly contribute to its continued success. As Panchami continues to evolve and innovate, it serves as an inspiring example for other businesses in the aromatherapy and alternative medicine industries, demonstrating the potential for growth and prosperity when tradition and innovation are seamlessly combined.

Tips for Spotting Untapped Potential with Real-Time Examples

In the highly competitive world of business, the ability to identify untapped potential in the market can be the key to success. Here are some tips to help you spot opportunities and capitalize on them, along with real-time examples:

1. Conduct thorough market research: The foundation for identifying untapped potential in any market lies in comprehensive market research. Analyze market trends, consumer preferences, and competitors' strategies to gain valuable insights into gaps and opportunities in the market. Example: Netflix identified the growing demand for on-demand streaming services through market research and capitalized on this untapped potential. Today, Netflix is a global leader in the streaming industry.

2. Listen to your customers: Your customers are the most valuable source of information when it comes to identifying untapped potential. Regularly engage with them through surveys, feedback forms, and social media to understand their needs and preferences. Example: Starbucks frequently engages with its customers to understand their preferences, leading to the introduction of new products like plant-based milk alternatives and seasonal beverages that cater to evolving consumer tastes.

3. Explore niche markets: Niche markets can offer untapped potential for businesses willing to cater to the unique needs of a specific customer segment. Identify and target niche markets to establish a strong presence before competitors enter the market. Example: Warby Parker recognized the niche market for affordable, stylish prescription eyewear and disrupted the traditional eyewear industry by offering a unique, direct-to-consumer business model.

4. Leverage technology and innovation: Adopting new technologies and embracing innovation can help you identify untapped potential in the market by offering unique solutions and products that cater to emerging consumer needs. Example: Tesla's focus on electric vehicles and innovative technologies has allowed it to establish itself as a leader in the sustainable transportation market, an area with significant untapped potential.

5. Observe successful businesses in other markets: Study successful businesses in other industries or countries to identify strategies, products, or services that can be adapted to your market. Example: Spotify entered the Indian market by observing the success of music streaming services in other countries and tailoring its offering to cater to local preferences, such as incorporating regional music and offering affordable subscription plans.

6. Pay attention to changing demographics: Demographic shifts, such as an aging population or increasing urbanization, can create untapped potential in the market. Analyze demographic trends and develop products or services that cater to the emerging needs of these demographic groups. Example: The growing aging population has led to increased demand for products and services that cater to seniors, such as home healthcare services and senior-friendly consumer products.

7. Capitalize on emerging trends: Keep an eye on emerging trends in your industry and be prepared to adapt your products or services to cater to these new developments. Example: Beyond Meat identified the growing trend of plant-based diets and

capitalized on this untapped potential by offering plant-based meat alternatives that appeal to both vegetarians and meat-eaters alike.

8. Seek strategic partnerships and collaborations: Collaborating with other businesses or organizations can help you identify untapped potential by combining resources, expertise, and market reach. Example: Uber Eats' partnership with McDonald's allowed the food delivery service to expand rapidly and tap into the potential of fast-food delivery, which was previously an underserved market.

9. Foster a culture of innovation within your organization: Encourage your team to think creatively and challenge the status quo. This can help your business identify untapped potential and develop innovative solutions to address market gaps. Example: Google's "20 percent time" policy, which allowed employees to spend a portion of their work time on personal projects, led to the development of innovative products like Gmail and Google Maps.

10. Be willing to take risks: Identifying and capitalizing on untapped potential often involves taking risks and venturing into uncharted territory. Be prepared to embrace change, learn from failures, and persevere in the face of obstacles. Example: Airbnb took a significant risk by entering the highly regulated hotel industry with its unique home-sharing model. Despite facing numerous challenges, the company persisted and is now a dominant player in the global travel market.

11. Monitor social and environmental trends: Social and environmental issues can drive consumer preferences and create untapped potential in the market. Stay informed about these trends and develop products or services that address these concerns. Example: Patagonia, an outdoor clothing company, recognized the growing concern for environmental sustainability and responded by creating eco-friendly products and promoting sustainable business practices. This approach has helped the company build a loyal customer base and differentiate itself in the crowded outdoor apparel market.

12. Be adaptable and agile: In a constantly changing market landscape, businesses need to be agile and adaptable to identify and capitalize on untapped potential. Be prepared to pivot your strategy, products, or services in response to new opportunities and challenges. Example: Adobe transitioned from selling packaged software to offering cloud-based software subscriptions, allowing the company to adapt to the changing needs of its customers and tap into the growing market for cloud services.

By incorporating these tips into your business strategy and staying attuned to the evolving market landscape, you can successfully identify and capitalize on untapped potential in your industry. Embrace innovation, be open to change, and continually seek opportunities to grow and evolve, ensuring long-term success in the competitive world of business.

4

AI: The Digital Revolution in Indian Businesses

Artificial Intelligence (AI), once a concept confined to the realms of science fiction, has now pervasively integrated into our daily lives and reshaped various sectors. Businesses worldwide are leveraging AI for improved efficiencies, better decision-making, and personalized customer experiences. India, with its rapidly growing digital economy, is not far behind.

The Emergence and Growth of AI

The development of AI technology can be traced back to the mid-20th century, but it has experienced significant growth and advancement in recent years. AI combines machine learning, natural language processing, deep learning, and robotics to simulate human intelligence. Over time, AI has evolved from rule-based systems that could only perform basic tasks to learning-based systems capable of complex problem-solving and predictive analysis.

In today's society, AI is omnipresent. It's found in every corner of our world, from digital voice assistants like Siri and Alexa to Google's search algorithms, Netflix's personalized recommendations, and even self-driving cars. AI has become an integral part of our daily lives.

AI in the Business World

AI has the potential to revolutionize the business world by automating tasks, analyzing vast amounts of data, identifying trends, and providing insights that humans may overlook. Many companies use AI to enhance productivity, improve customer service, and make informed decisions.

One of the primary applications of AI is predictive analytics, which enables businesses to forecast future trends based on historical data. This allows them to strategize better and gain a competitive edge. AI-powered customer service bots are another popular application, providing 24/7 assistance to customers and resulting in increased satisfaction and loyalty.

AI also helps in personalizing the user experience. By analyzing consumer behavior and preferences, businesses can deliver personalized content and recommendations, thus enhancing the customer journey and increasing conversion rates.

AI's Growing Relevance in India

In India, AI's relevance has grown substantially in recent years. Digital transformation and increased internet penetration have catalyzed the adoption of AI across various sectors, including healthcare, agriculture, education, finance, and e-commerce.

AI-powered applications are being used to diagnose diseases, predict crop yield, personalize learning, detect fraudulent transactions, and enhance the online shopping experience. In agriculture, for instance, AI-enabled drones are used for crop monitoring, while AI-powered platforms provide farmers with insights on weather conditions, soil health, and pest infestation.

India, with its massive population and diversity, presents a unique set of challenges and opportunities for AI. The availability of vast amounts of data, coupled with a growing tech-savvy population and a supportive government policy framework, makes India a fertile ground for AI innovations.

Looking Forward

Despite the challenges of infrastructure, data privacy, and the digital divide, the future of AI in India looks promising. The government's National Strategy for AI and the setting up of centers of excellence for AI research and development are steps in the right direction.

Indian start-ups are leveraging AI to address India-specific problems, thus driving social impact. AI-powered solutions are helping in areas like traffic management, waste disposal, and skill development, showcasing the immense potential of AI to drive societal change.

With the growth of AI, new job roles like data scientist, AI engineer, and AI ethicist have emerged, indicating a shift in the skills required in the future job market. While there are concerns about job losses due to automation, it's important to view AI as a tool that can augment human capabilities rather than replace them.

Advantages and Disadvantages of AI in Business: A Global and Indian Perspective

The Upside of AI in Business

Artificial Intelligence (AI) brings a wealth of advantages to businesses, opening the gateway to unprecedented efficiencies, innovation, and competitive advantages.

Increased Efficiency and Productivity: By automating routine and mundane tasks, AI allows employees to focus on more complex and creative aspects of their work. For instance, chatbots can manage customer inquiries, while AI-driven algorithms can handle data analysis, reducing the burden on human resources and increasing overall productivity.

Better Decision-Making: AI's ability to process and analyze vast amounts of data quickly allows for more informed and timely decision-making. Predictive analytics, one form of AI, helps businesses anticipate market trends, customer behavior, and potential operational issues.

Enhanced Customer Experience: AI enables personalization at scale. From personalized product recommendations to targeted marketing, AI technologies deliver experiences tailored to individual customer preferences, driving engagement and loyalty.

Innovation and Competitive Advantage: Businesses adopting AI can offer innovative services and products, gaining a significant edge over competitors. From autonomous vehicles to AI-powered health diagnostics, organizations at the forefront of AI are revolutionizing industries.

Indian Perspective: In India, where businesses often grapple with resource constraints, AI can bring immense value. For example, AI can help Indian farmers through predictive analytics for weather and soil conditions, thus increasing crop yields. Similarly, AI can provide affordable and accessible healthcare solutions by assisting with diagnosis and treatment recommendations.

The Downside of AI in Business

Despite its transformative potential, AI also brings challenges and risks that businesses must address to avoid pitfalls.

High Initial Costs: Implementing AI technologies requires substantial upfront investment in infrastructure, talent acquisition, and training, which may be prohibitive for small and medium-sized businesses.

Data Privacy and Security Concerns: AI systems rely on extensive data, raising concerns about data privacy and security. Unauthorized access to data, misuse of personal information, or algorithmic bias can lead to significant reputational harm and legal issues.

Job Displacement Fears: The automation of tasks by AI technologies creates concerns about job displacement, especially for roles involving routine tasks. Businesses must address these concerns proactively through reskilling and upskilling initiatives.

Reliability and Accountability Issues: AI systems, while advanced, are not infallible and can make mistakes. There can also be a lack of clarity about accountability when AI-driven systems fail or cause harm.

Indian Perspective: In India, challenges include the digital divide, lack of AI awareness, and shortage of AI-skilled talent. Many Indian businesses are still in the early stages of digital transformation, and adoption of AI is uneven across sectors. There are also concerns about data privacy, given India's vast population and the lack of a comprehensive data protection law.

The Path Ahead

The global and Indian business landscapes present both enormous opportunities and significant challenges for AI. Businesses must navigate these carefully, balancing the pursuit of innovation with ethical considerations and societal impacts.

The businesses that will emerge as leaders in the AI era will be those that can effectively leverage the benefits of AI, address its risks, and remain responsive to evolving regulatory frameworks and societal expectations. In India, businesses that can use AI to address India-specific challenges will not only gain a competitive advantage but also drive inclusive growth and societal progress.

AI is not just a technological revolution; it is a business revolution. The way businesses respond to this revolution will shape their trajectories and influence the wider economic and social landscape.

The Ethical Perspective of AI

Beyond the advantages and disadvantages, it's also crucial to consider AI from an ethical perspective. AI, like any powerful tool, can be used for both beneficial and harmful purposes. It's important for businesses to use AI responsibly, considering its potential impacts on individuals and society.

The most evident ethical concern with AI involves privacy and consent. Businesses that use AI to analyze consumer behavior have a responsibility to protect user data and use it ethically. This includes informing users about how their data is being used and giving them the option to opt out if they wish.

Algorithmic bias is another ethical issue. AI systems learn from data, and if the data is biased, the AI system's output will also be biased. This can lead to discriminatory practices, affecting minority and disadvantaged groups disproportionately. Therefore, it's vital to use diverse datasets and regularly check AI systems for bias.

In India, with its diverse population and cultural nuances, ethical AI implementation requires extra consideration. Given the digital divide, there's a risk that AI could exacerbate existing inequalities. It's crucial for businesses to ensure that the benefits of AI are accessible to all sections of society, not just the privileged few.

Preparing for the AI Future

Despite the challenges, the future of AI in business looks bright, both globally and in India. Businesses that embrace AI will likely lead the pack, while those that resist may fall behind.

Preparing for this future requires a strategic approach. Here are some steps businesses can take:

Invest in AI Infrastructure: This includes both technical infrastructure (like data storage and processing capabilities) and human infrastructure (like hiring AI specialists or training existing staff).

Develop an AI Strategy: Businesses need to identify how AI can best serve their needs. This might involve using AI to improve customer service, streamline operations, or develop new products or services.

Establish Data Management Practices: Businesses need robust data management practices to protect privacy, ensure security, and comply with regulations.

Prioritize Ethics and Responsibility: This includes considering the ethical implications of AI, implementing measures to prevent bias, and ensuring transparency and accountability.

Stay Informed About AI Developments: AI is a rapidly evolving field, and it's important to stay up-to-date on new technologies, best practices, and regulatory changes.

Indian Perspective: In India, businesses also need to consider the specific Indian context. This might involve adapting AI technologies to work with Indian languages and cultural practices, addressing the digital divide, and complying with Indian regulations.

Conclusion

AI in business is more than just a trend – it's a transformative force that's reshaping the business landscape. While AI brings many benefits, it also brings challenges and risks. Businesses need to approach AI with a balanced perspective, recognizing both its potential and its pitfalls.

In the end, successful AI adoption isn't just about technology – it's about using technology in a way that aligns with business goals, societal values, and ethical principles. This will be the key to unlocking AI's full potential in business, both globally and in India.

AI: Driving Growth for Small and Medium Businesses

Artificial Intelligence (AI) is not exclusive to large corporations; it holds transformative potential for small and medium businesses (SMBs) as well. SMBs form the backbone of many economies, including India, and the adoption of AI can play a significant role in their growth and sustainability.

Efficient Operations

AI can automate many day-to-day tasks, leading to increased efficiency and productivity. For instance, AI-powered software can handle tasks like bookkeeping, invoice generation, inventory management, and customer service, freeing up time for SMB owners to focus on core business activities.

AI can also optimize supply chain operations. For example, AI can predict demand patterns, helping SMBs optimize their inventory, thereby reducing storage costs and improving customer satisfaction.

Data-Driven Decisions

AI-powered analytics tools can provide SMBs with valuable insights into their business operations and customer behavior. These insights can guide decision-making, from pricing strategies to marketing campaigns and from product development to customer service improvements.

Personalized Marketing

AI can help SMBs understand their customers on a deeper level. By analyzing customer behavior and preferences, AI can enable personalized marketing, enhancing customer engagement and loyalty. AI can also optimize advertising expenditure by identifying the most effective channels and times for marketing campaigns.

Customer Service Enhancement

AI-powered chatbots can provide 24/7 customer support, answering common queries and freeing up staff for more complex customer interactions. These chatbots can improve response times and customer satisfaction, which is crucial for SMBs to compete with larger businesses.

Indian Perspective

In India, where SMBs form a significant part of the economy, the benefits of AI are particularly relevant. Given India's vast consumer base and diverse market segments, AI can help Indian SMBs understand their customers better and tailor their offerings accordingly.

AI can also help Indian SMBs overcome resource constraints. For instance, AI-powered EdTech platforms can provide affordable and effective training for SMB employees, addressing skill gaps and enhancing productivity.

Overcoming Barriers to AI Adoption

Despite the potential benefits, some barriers might deter SMBs from adopting AI. These include the perceived high cost of AI technologies, lack of awareness about AI, and lack of AI-related skills.

To overcome these barriers, it's crucial to increase awareness about the benefits of AI and the range of AI solutions available, including those tailored for SMBs. Businesses can also access AI skills through partnerships, outsourcing, or online training platforms.

Governments and industry bodies can play a role, too, by providing funding support for AI adoption, creating AI training programs, and developing guidelines to ensure ethical and responsible AI use.

Conclusion

The integration of AI in business is no longer a futuristic concept; it's a reality that's reshaping the business landscape today. For SMBs, AI adoption is not just about staying competitive - it's a crucial enabler of growth and innovation.

AI can help SMBs become more efficient, make informed decisions, personalize their marketing, and enhance their customer service. In India, the adoption of AI by SMBs can drive not just business growth but also broader economic and social development.

Embracing AI might seem daunting for some SMBs, but with the right approach and support, the journey can be rewarding. The future of SMBs is inextricably linked with AI, and those that recognize this will be well-placed to thrive in the evolving business ecosystem.

AI Innovation and New Market Opportunities

Beyond operational improvements and efficiencies, AI also opens up new avenues for innovation and market opportunities for SMBs.

Product and Service Innovation

AI can foster innovation in product and service offerings. For instance, SMBs in the healthcare sector can leverage AI for personalized wellness recommendations or early diagnosis systems. In the retail sector, AI can be used to develop personalized shopping experiences using augmented reality or virtual reality.

Expanding Market Reach

Digital platforms powered by AI can enable SMBs to reach customers beyond their immediate geographical area. AI-powered e-commerce platforms can recommend products to a global audience, significantly expanding the market reach of SMBs.

Real-Time Business Adaptation

AI systems can process and react to real-time data, allowing businesses to adapt quickly to changes. This agility can be a significant competitive advantage for SMBs, allowing them to seize new opportunities or mitigate challenges promptly.

Indian Perspective

In India, AI can help SMBs address several unique market challenges and opportunities. For instance, India has several regional languages, and AI can be used to develop translation tools or multilingual customer service bots, allowing SMBs to cater to customers across different regions.

In sectors like agriculture or handloom, where many SMBs operate, AI can provide weather predictions, crop disease detection, design assistance, and global market access, transforming traditional sectors with modern technology.

Toward an AI-Positive Future

Adopting AI is not without challenges. It involves a learning curve and necessitates changes in business processes and culture. However, the benefits can far outweigh the investment in the long run.

Here are some strategies for SMBs to navigate their AI journey:

Begin with the End in Mind: Define clear goals and metrics for your AI projects. What business problem are you trying to solve? What benefits do you expect? This clarity can guide your AI journey.

Start Small, Think Big: Start with small AI projects to gain familiarity and confidence. As your skills and experience grow, you can take on larger and more ambitious projects.

Collaborate and Learn: Collaboration can be a powerful strategy for SMBs. Collaborate with technology providers, join industry groups, and learn from others' experiences.

Invest in Skills and Culture: Make AI a part of your business culture. Encourage continuous learning and innovation among your team.

Indian Perspective: For Indian SMBs, collaborating with local AI startups and leveraging government initiatives for AI skill development can be effective strategies. Additionally, given the diversity of India, considering regional and cultural nuances in AI projects is essential.

Conclusion

The possibilities for SMBs with AI are vast and exciting. From transforming operations to enabling innovation and expanding market reach, AI holds the potential to drive significant growth for SMBs.

For Indian SMBs, AI is more than a business tool - it's a catalyst for societal progress, helping traditional sectors modernize and enabling businesses to reach and serve a diverse population better.

The AI revolution in business is here, and SMBs - the backbone of many economies - have a pivotal role in this revolution. With a strategic and thoughtful approach to AI adoption, SMBs can not only thrive in the AI era but also shape it in a way that aligns with their values and aspirations.

AI Applications for Automating Tasks: Practical Examples

Artificial Intelligence is a powerful tool for automating tasks, allowing businesses to improve efficiency, reduce errors, and free up time for more strategic activities. Here are some practical examples of AI applications in task automation.

Administrative Tasks

One of the most straightforward applications of AI in automation is administrative tasks.

For instance, AI-powered software can handle tasks such as scheduling meetings, sorting and replying to emails, or managing calendars. This can free up a significant amount of time for business owners and employees.

Example: Clara, an AI-powered virtual employee, can schedule meetings, send reminders, and even reschedule appointments when necessary.

Customer Service

AI can automate several aspects of customer service, from answering common queries to handling complaints.

Example: Chatbots, like those used by Domino's Pizza, can process orders, provide updates, and answer queries, providing customers with immediate responses and freeing up time for human staff to handle more complex queries.

Data Analysis

AI can automate data analysis, turning large volumes of data into actionable insights.

Example: Tableau's AI-powered analytics can process large datasets, identify trends and patterns, and present them in easy-to-understand visual formats, saving businesses the time and effort of manual data analysis.

HR and Recruitment

AI can automate several HR tasks, from screening resumes to scheduling interviews and even gauging candidate suitability through sentiment analysis.

Example: HireVue's AI system can analyze video interviews to assess candidates' language, tone, and facial expressions, providing insights that go beyond what's on the resume.

Marketing

AI can automate several aspects of marketing, from segmenting customers and personalizing content to optimizing advertising campaigns.

Example: Marketo, a marketing automation platform, uses AI to predict the best times and channels to engage with customers, improving marketing effectiveness and efficiency.

Indian Perspective

In India, AI is being used to automate tasks in various sectors. For instance, in agriculture, AI can automate crop monitoring, predict diseases, and suggest optimal harvesting times.

Example: Fasal, an Indian AgriTech startup, uses AI to provide real-time actionable insights to farmers, such as when to water, feed, and harvest crops, automating complex decision-making processes.

Empowering SMBs through AI: Enhancing Digital Presence

In today's digital-first world, a robust online presence is crucial for small and medium-sized businesses (SMBs). AI tools and platforms can help SMBs enhance their digital presence, engage with customers more effectively, and drive business growth.

Social Media Marketing

AI can automate and optimize various aspects of social media marketing.

For instance, AI tools can analyze social media data to identify trends, optimize posting times, and personalize content for different customer segments. AI can also help with sentiment analysis, allowing businesses to understand and respond to customer emotions effectively.

Example: Buffer is a social media management tool that uses AI to determine optimal posting times, increasing the visibility of posts.

Search Engine Optimization (SEO)

SEO is crucial for SMBs to increase their online visibility. AI can help optimize website content for search engines, improving search rankings and attracting more organic traffic.

Example: BrightEdge is an AI-powered SEO platform that provides real-time insights and recommendations to improve website ranking.

Website Personalization

AI can personalize website content based on visitor behavior and preferences, improving user engagement and conversion rates.

Example: OneSpot is an AI-powered platform that personalizes website content in real-time, creating a unique and engaging experience for each visitor.

Customer Journey Optimization

AI can analyze customer behavior across different digital channels and touchpoints (the 'customer journey'), helping businesses understand and improve their customer experience.

Example: Mid-journey is an AI-driven marketing platform that helps businesses understand their customer's journey and optimize their marketing strategies accordingly.

Predictive Analytics

AI can use past data to predict future behavior, helping businesses anticipate customer needs, optimize their offerings, and make informed business decisions.

Example: Salesforce Einstein is an AI-powered tool that provides predictive insights, helping businesses forecast sales, identify high-value customers, and predict customer churn.

Chatbots and Virtual Assistants

AI-powered chatbots and virtual assistants can handle customer queries, provide product information, and even process transactions, providing 24/7 customer support and freeing up time for human staff.

Example: ManyChat is a platform that helps SMBs build chatbots for Facebook Messenger, improving customer engagement and support.

Indian Perspective

In India, several AI tools and platforms are helping SMBs enhance their digital presence.

Example: Vernacular.ai, an Indian startup, provides AI-powered voice assistants that can interact with customers in various Indian languages, helping SMBs cater to a diverse customer base.

Conclusion

For SMBs, enhancing their digital presence is not just about having a website or being on social media; it's about engaging with customers effectively, personalizing their experience, and understanding their journey. With AI, SMBs can achieve this at scale, driving customer engagement, loyalty, and business growth.

In the Indian context, AI can help SMBs cater to a diverse and fast-evolving digital consumer base, enabling them to thrive in India's vibrant digital economy. By embracing AI, Indian SMBs can not just participate in the digital revolution but also shape it in a way that aligns with their aspirations and values.

While AI can automate many tasks, it's not without challenges. These include data privacy concerns, potential job displacement, and the need for continuous monitoring and updating of AI systems. Businesses need to address these challenges proactively and ethically to make the most of AI automation.

Case studies of successful AI adoption in India

1. Case Study: ZestMoney - AI in Financial Services

Background

ZestMoney is a Bengaluru-based fintech startup that offers EMI (equated monthly installments) without credit cards to Indian consumers. Founded in 2015, the company partners with financial institutions to provide small ticket loans for online purchases.

AI Adoption

ZestMoney integrates AI into its core operations. The AI system is utilized to assess the creditworthiness of customers, many of whom lack a formal credit history, which is a common scenario in India.

The AI model analyzes a diverse range of data, including financial transactions, mobile usage, social media activities, and other alternative data, to generate a credit score. This enables ZestMoney to offer loans to customers who are often overlooked by traditional banks.

ZestMoney also employs AI to automate customer service, using chatbots to address customer queries, provide updates, and process loan applications, thus enhancing efficiency and improving customer experience.

Impact

ZestMoney's AI-driven approach has resulted in significant business growth. As of 2022, the company had over 11 million registered users and had partnered with more than 3,000 online and offline merchants.

By using AI to assess creditworthiness, ZestMoney is promoting financial inclusion and democratizing access to credit in India.

Lessons Learned

ZestMoney's success exemplifies the potential of AI in transforming traditional sectors like finance. By harnessing AI, businesses can innovate their offerings, serve underserved markets, and drive growth.

2. Case Study: Ninjacart - AI in Agriculture

Background

Ninjacart is a Bengaluru-based agritech startup that connects farmers with retailers through a tech-driven supply chain. Founded in 2015, Ninjacart aims to reduce food wastage and increase farmers' earnings.

AI Adoption

Ninjacart uses AI in several ways. One crucial application is in logistics, where AI algorithms determine the most efficient routes for delivery, considering factors like traffic, weather, and delivery slots.

The AI system also predicts demand for different products based on historical data, weather, and market trends, helping farmers decide what to plant.

Moreover, Ninjacart uses AI to automate quality checks. Images of produce are analyzed by AI to determine the quality, reducing manual effort and improving accuracy.

Impact

Ninjacart has successfully reduced food wastage and increased the efficiency of its supply chain through AI. As of 2022, Ninjacart was moving over 1,400 tonnes of produce daily, serving over 60,000 retailers, and had a network of more than 20,000 farmers.

By leveraging AI, Ninjacart is transforming India's agriculture sector, making it more efficient, sustainable, and profitable for farmers.

Lessons Learned

Ninjacart's experience shows how AI can solve complex, real-world problems like food wastage and supply chain inefficiency. The key is to understand the problem deeply, collect the right data and develop AI models that can handle the complexity and variability of the real world.

These examples should give you a taste of what AI can achieve in the Indian context. The remaining case studies would cover other sectors and applications, highlighting the versatility and impact of AI across the Indian business landscape.

3. Case Study: Curefit - AI in Healthcare and Wellness

Background

Curefit is a Bengaluru-based health and wellness startup. Founded in 2016, Curefit provides a holistic approach to health and wellness, including fitness, nutrition, mental health, and primary care.

AI Adoption

Curefit leverages AI to deliver personalized health and fitness experiences. For example, their mobile app uses AI algorithms to create personalized workout plans and meal plans based on individual users' health data, fitness goals, and preferences.

Curefit's mental wellness platform, Mindfit, uses AI to offer personalized meditation and yoga programs. AI is also used to power their customer service chatbots, answering queries and offering support 24/7.

In addition, during the COVID-19 pandemic, Curefit launched an AI-powered tool to assess the risk of COVID-19 based on users' symptoms and travel history.

Impact

Curefit's AI-driven approach has led to substantial business growth. As of 2023, Curefit has over 1.5 million active users and has expanded into several international markets.

By providing personalized, convenient, and affordable health and wellness services, Curefit is promoting healthier lifestyles and improving health outcomes.

Lessons Learned

Curefit's success demonstrates the power of AI in personalized health and wellness services. By leveraging AI, businesses can deliver personalized experiences at scale, improving customer satisfaction and business outcomes.

4. Case Study: SigTuple - AI in Healthcare Diagnostics

Background

Founded in 2015, SigTuple is a health tech startup based in Bengaluru that is revolutionizing healthcare diagnostics through AI. SigTuple creates intelligent screening solutions to aid diagnosis through AI-powered analysis of visual medical data.

AI Adoption

SigTuple has developed AI algorithms that can analyze medical images and detect abnormalities. Its flagship product, Manthana, uses

AI to analyze peripheral blood smears and retinal scans, among other medical images.

The platform has the capability to detect conditions such as anemia, malaria, and diabetic retinopathy, usually in a fraction of the time it would take a human specialist. It not only increases diagnostic speed but also standardizes the quality of diagnosis across different labs and hospitals.

Impact

SigTuple's AI-based solutions provide a faster, less expensive, and more accurate diagnosis, which is particularly beneficial in rural areas where access to medical specialists may be limited. As of 2023, SigTuple's solutions have been used in over a thousand diagnostic labs across India.

By making medical diagnostics faster, cheaper, and more accessible, SigTuple is democratizing access to quality healthcare in India.

Lessons Learned

SigTuple's experience shows that AI can improve the quality, speed, and accessibility of healthcare. The key is to develop AI models that can analyze complex medical data accurately and consistently and to work closely with healthcare professionals to ensure that AI solutions meet their needs and the needs of the patients.

5. Case Study: CropIn - AI in AgriTech

Background

CropIn is a Bangalore-based startup providing AI and data-led solutions for agribusinesses. Founded in 2010, CropIn aims to make farming more sustainable and productive, benefiting farmers, businesses, and the environment.

AI Adoption

CropIn leverages AI and machine learning to analyze diverse datasets, including satellite imagery, weather data, and on-field data captured by farmers. This data is then used to provide predictive insights on crop yields, pest infestations, and the ideal time for harvesting.

Moreover, their SmartFarm platform uses AI to help farmers optimize their farm management. It provides advice on the best crops to plant based on weather forecasts, soil health, and market demand.

Impact

CropIn's technology is currently being used by hundreds of agribusinesses worldwide, reaching over 3 million acres and benefiting over 2 million farmers. This has resulted in a significant increase in crop yields, reduced use of water and chemicals, and improved sustainability.

Lessons Learned

The success of CropIn shows the vast potential for AI in agriculture, particularly in a country like India, where farming is a major part of the economy. By leveraging AI, it's possible to make agriculture more productive, sustainable, and profitable, all while addressing global challenges like food security and climate change.

6. Case Study: Staqu - AI in Fashion and E-commerce

Background

Staqu is a Gurugram-based startup that uses AI to enhance the shopping experience in the fashion and e-commerce industry.

Founded in 2015, Staqu provides image-to-image search technology, allowing users to find products by simply uploading a photo.

AI Adoption

Staqu's AI solution, known as Fashion, uses image recognition technology to analyze clothing items in any given image. When users upload an image or select a picture of a celebrity from their gallery, the AI recognizes the clothes in the photo and suggests similar items available online, along with price comparisons.

Beyond fashion, Staqu has also used its AI expertise in other areas, such as assisting the police force with facial recognition technology.

Impact

Staqu's unique AI-powered solution has been implemented by several e-commerce platforms in India, improving the shopping experience for millions of users. The adoption of AI by Staqu has helped the startup gain a substantial foothold in the booming e-commerce market of India.

Lessons Learned

Staqu's journey demonstrates how AI can be used to create unique, innovative solutions that disrupt traditional industries. By thinking outside the box and leveraging AI, businesses can create new value for their customers, differentiating themselves from the competition.

7. Case Study: Karza Technologies - AI in Banking and Finance

Background

Karza Technologies is a Mumbai-based fintech company that provides banking and business solutions using AI and big data analytics.

Founded in 2015, Karza aims to help businesses manage risk and make informed decisions.

AI Adoption

Karza has developed AI algorithms that analyze diverse data sets to generate risk profiles for potential customers or investments. For example, their bank statement analyzer can generate a risk profile in seconds, using AI to assess patterns in income, spending, and late payments.

Their AI-based systems also help businesses verify the authenticity of documents, automate credit assessments, and provide insights into potential market opportunities.

Impact

Karza's AI-driven solutions have been adopted by over 300 financial institutions across India. They have helped businesses streamline operations, make more informed decisions, and significantly reduce the risk of fraud.

Lessons Learned

Karza Technologies exemplifies how AI can transform traditional sectors like banking and finance. By adopting AI, businesses can not only automate routine tasks but also generate insights that help them make more informed decisions.

8. Case Study: Tricog - AI in Healthcare

Background

Tricog is a health tech startup based in Bangalore. Founded in 2015, Tricog provides AI-based solutions to help doctors diagnose and treat heart disease.

AI Adoption

Tricog has developed an AI system that can analyze ECG data in real time. By identifying patterns that indicate heart disease, the system can help doctors diagnose conditions like heart attacks much more quickly, often within minutes.

Moreover, Tricog's AI system is cloud-based, allowing it to be used anywhere in the world. This means it can assist doctors in remote areas who may not have access to a cardiologist.

Impact

Tricog's AI solution is currently used by doctors in over 3,000 clinics across India. It has helped diagnose tens of thousands of cases of heart disease, potentially saving many lives.

Lessons Learned

Tricog's journey shows that AI can make a real difference in people's lives by improving healthcare outcomes. By using AI, we can overcome the limitations of traditional healthcare systems and provide high-quality care to people everywhere.

These case studies illustrate the diverse applications of AI across different sectors in India, demonstrating how AI can drive innovation, efficiency, and growth in the Indian market. As AI continues to evolve, it will undoubtedly play an even bigger role in shaping India's future.

9. Case Study: BigBasket - AI in Retail

Background

BigBasket is India's largest online food and grocery store, based in Bengaluru. Since its inception in 2011, BigBasket has significantly disrupted the grocery retail sector in India.

AI Adoption

BigBasket leverages AI in several ways to optimize its operations and improve customer experiences. For instance, it uses machine learning algorithms to forecast demand for different products. These predictions are based on historical sales data, upcoming events, and other relevant factors.

In addition, BigBasket uses AI to optimize its delivery routes. By analyzing traffic data and other variables, the AI system can determine the fastest route for each delivery, reducing delivery times and fuel consumption.

Furthermore, the company uses AI to personalize customer experiences. For example, their recommendation system uses AI to suggest products that a customer may like based on their browsing and purchase history.

Impact

BigBasket's use of AI has led to significant improvements in efficiency, customer satisfaction, and business growth. As of 2023, BigBasket serves millions of customers across India and has a 35% market share in the online grocery segment.

Lessons Learned

BigBasket's story illustrates how AI can be a game-changer in the retail sector. By using AI to predict demand, optimize deliveries, and personalize experiences, retailers can enhance customer satisfaction, improve operational efficiency, and drive growth.

10. Case Study: NextWealth - AI in BPO and IT Services

Background

NextWealth Entrepreneurs is a unique organization that promotes digital entrepreneurship in smaller towns across India. Started in 2011, NextWealth leverages AI and digital technology to create jobs and promote entrepreneurship.

AI Adoption

NextWealth uses AI to automate various BPO (Business Process Outsourcing) services. For example, they use AI-powered Optical Character Recognition (OCR) to digitize handwritten or printed documents. They also use AI to automate data entry, transcription services, and other routine tasks.

Impact

NextWealth's AI-powered services have not only made BPO services faster and more accurate, but they have also created thousands of jobs in smaller towns where job opportunities are often limited. As of 2023, NextWealth works with over 50 digital entrepreneurs and provides services to over 100 customers worldwide.

Lessons Learned

NextWealth shows that AI is not just about automating tasks and reducing costs. It can also be a tool for social good, creating jobs and promoting entrepreneurship. It shows that with the right approach, AI can benefit businesses, individuals, and society as a whole.

These case studies showcase the broad spectrum of AI applications in various sectors within India, highlighting how businesses have harnessed AI to drive innovation, streamline operations, and cultivate growth. As AI technology continues to evolve, its role in shaping India's business landscape is set to grow even further.

5

The Power of Social Media and Digital Marketing

Evolution of Social Media in India

Over the last decade, India's social media landscape has undergone an impressive transformation. Initially used as a means to connect with friends and family, social media has now become a crucial tool for businesses and marketers in India. This shift can be attributed to several factors, including higher internet penetration, the proliferation of smartphones, and changes in user behavior. In this section, we delve into the story of social media in India, examining its significant milestones and exploring its impact on businesses and society.

1. The early days of social media (2004-2008)

Social media's roots in India can be traced back to 2004, when Orkut was introduced. It quickly gained popularity among Indian users, allowing them to create profiles, join communities, and connect with friends. Hi5 and MySpace also gained some attention during this time. However, it was Facebook's launch in 2006 that truly pushed social media to new heights in India. Initially, Facebook was primarily used by urban youth to connect with friends, share photos, and play games. Twitter also entered the Indian market during this time, gaining popularity for its concise format and real-time information sharing.

During the early days of social media (2004-2008), Shaadi.com, an online matrimonial service, was among the pioneers in India utilizing social media platforms for business growth. Established in 1997, the company recognized the internet's potential to revolutionize the traditional arranged marriage system. As social media platforms like Orkut and Facebook gained popularity in the early 2000s, Shaadi.com effectively leveraged these platforms to engage with its target audience and expand its reach. By creating profiles and pages on social media, the company connected with potential users shared success stories, and positioned itself as a trustworthy platform for finding life partners.

To better serve its diverse customer base, Shaadi.com utilized social media to gain insight into users' preferences and gather feedback. By actively engaging with their audience and building trust and credibility, the platform experienced a growing user base and a stronger brand presence. Although Shaadi.com may not have had as much social media impact as later brands, their early adoption of digital marketing in India showcased the power of these platforms for business growth.

2. The rise of smartphones and internet penetration (2009-2012)

The rise of social media in India was largely fueled by the widespread adoption of smartphones and increased internet penetration. With affordable smartphones and cheaper data plans, users were able to access social media platforms on the go, leading to a massive surge in the user base for platforms like Facebook and Twitter. Additionally, new social media platforms like Instagram and Pinterest emerged, further diversifying the social media landscape in India and providing users with a unique way to share their experiences and interests.

During the same time period, the e-commerce platform Flipkart successfully capitalized on the trend of increased smartphone and internet usage by launching its mobile app in 2011. This move not only increased customer engagement but also attracted a new segment of users who primarily accessed the internet through their smartphones. This user-friendly app, combined with the affordability of smartphones and mobile internet plans, helped Flipkart attract millions of new customers, especially from Tier 2 and Tier 3 cities where traditional brick-and-mortar retail was not as prevalent.

To ensure a seamless shopping experience for its customers, Flipkart invested heavily in its logistics and supply chain infrastructure. This, combined with innovative marketing strategies like the Big Billion Days sale, which generated massive buzz on social media, contributed to Flipkart's rapid growth and positioned it as one of the leading e-commerce platforms in India.

Overall, the rise of smartphones and internet penetration in India has led to a significant transformation in the tech industry, with social media and e-commerce platforms leveraging these trends to reach new heights. As technology continues to evolve and become more accessible, we can expect to see even more innovation and growth in the years to come.

3. The emergence of messaging apps and local platforms (2013-2016)

The rise of messaging apps like WhatsApp, WeChat, and Hike marked the next phase in the evolution of social media in India. These apps allowed users to communicate with friends and family through text, voice, and video, leading to a shift in user behavior. WhatsApp, in particular, gained immense popularity in India due to its simplicity and end-to-end encryption, which ensured secure communication.

During this period, several local social media platforms also emerged, catering to the unique needs and preferences of Indian users. For instance, platforms like ShareChat and Roposo provide content in regional languages, allowing users from diverse linguistic backgrounds to connect and share content.

During the period of 2013-2016, Hike Messenger, an Indian messaging app, successfully scaled by capitalizing on the emergence of messaging apps and local platforms. Launched in 2012 by Kavin Bharti Mittal, Hike Messenger quickly gained traction among Indian users thanks to its focus on localization and understanding the unique needs of the Indian market.

One of the key differentiating factors of Hike Messenger was its support for multiple Indian languages, which catered to the linguistic diversity of the country. This feature attracted millions of users who were more comfortable using messaging apps in their native languages.

In addition to language support, Hike Messenger introduced various localized features, such as Hike Stickers, which were designed to cater to the cultural nuances of the Indian audience. These stickers enabled users to express themselves more effectively, using popular Indian catchphrases and cultural references.

Hike Messenger also tapped into the popularity of local platforms by integrating services like news, games, live cricket scores, and more, turning the messaging app into a one-stop shop for its users' digital needs. This strategy helped Hike Messenger stand out among its competitors and gain a loyal user base.

Furthermore, the company focused on data-saving features, understanding the concerns of its target audience, who were often on limited data plans. Hike Messenger offered features like data compression, offline messaging, and the ability to send and receive messages without an active internet connection, catering to users in areas with limited network coverage.

By focusing on localization and understanding the unique needs of the Indian market, Hike Messenger was able to scale rapidly during the period of 2013-2016, reaching over 100 million registered users and becoming one of the top messaging apps in India.

4. The rise of video-sharing platforms and influencer culture (2017-present)

The recent years have witnessed remarkable growth in the popularity of short-form video content, thanks to the emergence of video-sharing platforms such as YouTube, Instagram's IGTV, and the now-banned TikTok in India. These platforms have given rise to a new generation of content creators and influencers who have amassed a significant following on social media.

The rise of short-form video content can be attributed to the introduction of Reliance Jio in 2016, which revolutionized the telecom market with its affordable data plans. This led to a surge in video consumption and the growth of platforms like TikTok, which gained millions of users in a short span of time. The influencer culture has also played a pivotal role in the rise of influencer marketing, where brands collaborate with social media personalities to promote their products and services. This has become a crucial aspect of digital marketing strategies for businesses across industries.

One company that has successfully leveraged the power of video-sharing platforms and influencer culture is Nykaa, an Indian fashion and beauty e-commerce platform. Founded by Falguni Nayar in 2012, Nykaa started as an online cosmetics retailer and quickly expanded to offer a wide range of beauty, wellness, and fashion products.

Nykaa capitalized on the influencer culture by partnering with popular beauty and fashion influencers on platforms like Instagram, YouTube, and TikTok (now banned in India). These influencers created engaging makeup tutorials and product reviews, showcasing Nykaa's products and driving engagement and brand awareness among their followers.

To further strengthen its brand image and appeal to a broader audience, Nykaa launched its own line of beauty products, which were often endorsed by influencers and celebrities. This helped to boost the credibility of the brand and establish Nykaa as a trusted name in the beauty and wellness industry.

In addition to influencer collaborations, Nykaa launched its own content platform called Nykaa TV, featuring beauty and fashion-related videos created by in-house experts and well-known influencers. This platform attracted millions of viewers, further driving traffic to their e-commerce site and boosting sales.

Nykaa also organized beauty and fashion events, inviting influencers and celebrities to participate in panel discussions, workshops, and other activities. These events generated significant buzz on social media, leading to an increased interest in the brand and its offerings.

By leveraging the power of video-sharing platforms and influencer culture, Nykaa has been able to scale rapidly, becoming one of the leading e-commerce platforms for beauty, wellness, and fashion in India. In 2021, the company went public, and its market valuation surpassed $13 billion, further demonstrating the success of its marketing strategies and its strong position in the Indian market.

The success of Nykaa's marketing strategies highlights the importance of adapting to the changing landscape of digital marketing and staying ahead of the curve. With the rise of short-form video content and influencer culture, businesses must embrace new and innovative marketing strategies to stay relevant and capture the attention of their target audience.

5. Impact on Businesses and Society

The evolution of social media in India has had a profound impact on businesses, society, and even individuals. With the power of social media, businesses can easily reach out to their target audience, engage with customers, and build brand awareness. Even small businesses and entrepreneurs can now promote their products and services at a fraction of the cost of traditional marketing methods.

Social media has not only been beneficial for businesses, but it has also played a crucial role in shaping public opinion and driving social change. From raising awareness about important issues and mobilizing support for various causes to giving a voice to marginalized communities, social media has become a powerful tool for advocacy and activism.

Moreover, the rise of social media has also created new career opportunities in the field of digital marketing, content creation, and influencer management. Young Indians are pursuing careers as social media managers, content creators, and influencers, working independently or as part of digital marketing agencies.

Social media has provided a platform for local businesses to showcase their products and services to a wider audience. One such example is Chumbak, a homegrown lifestyle brand that started in Bangalore in 2010. They used social media to promote their unique and quirky designs, which resonated with the Indian audience. Their social media strategy included creating engaging content, partnering with influencers, and hosting social media contests. This led to increased brand awareness, customer engagement, and, ultimately, increased sales. Today, Chumbak has over 40 stores across India and continues to expand both online and offline.

However, social media can also have a negative impact on businesses, especially when it comes to small businesses. For example, traditional Indian craftsmen and artisans have been struggling to survive in the age of social media. With the rise of online marketplaces and e-commerce platforms, many consumers have started to prefer mass-produced goods over handmade products. This has resulted in a decline in demand for traditional Indian crafts and has put many small businesses out of business. Despite this, some craftsmen have adapted to the digital age and have started to use social media platforms to showcase their unique products to a wider audience. This has allowed them to continue their craft and reach new customers who appreciate traditional Indian art and culture.

Dunzo is a hyperlocal delivery startup that has become popular in major Indian cities like Bangalore, Delhi, and Mumbai. The company provides delivery services for a wide range of products, including food, groceries, and medicine. Dunzo's success can largely be attributed to its effective use of social media. The company has a strong presence on platforms like Twitter and Instagram, where it engages with customers and shares updates about its services. By using social media to reach a wider audience and build a loyal following, Dunzo has been able to rapidly grow its user base and establish itself as a leader in the hyperlocal delivery space.

However, there are also instances where social media has put traditional businesses out of business in India. One example is the impact of e-commerce platforms like Amazon and Flipkart on small, traditional retail businesses. With the rise of online shopping in India, many small retailers have struggled to compete with the convenience and affordability of e-commerce platforms.

Despite this, many traditional businesses have also adapted to the changing landscape by embracing digital marketing and e-commerce themselves. For example, many small retailers have established an online presence by creating their own e-commerce websites or selling their products on platforms like Amazon and Flipkart. By leveraging social media and other digital marketing channels, these businesses have been able to stay competitive and continue to thrive in the changing Indian market.

In conclusion, the evolution of social media has brought about both positive and negative impacts on businesses and society in India. While it has provided a platform for businesses to reach out to their target audience more effectively, it has also posed challenges for traditional businesses. Nonetheless, those who have adapted to the digital age have been able to thrive and succeed in the changing Indian market.

6. Challenges and the future of social media in India

Social media has undoubtedly brought about a significant impact on India's digital landscape. With over 450 million users, it has become an integral part of everyday life, connecting people from different corners of the country. However, despite its positive contributions, social media also poses several challenges that need to be addressed.

One of the most significant challenges is the spread of fake news, which can have severe consequences in a country as diverse as India. Misinformation can spread like wildfire and trigger communal tensions, leading to violence and unrest. The Indian government has taken several steps to tackle this issue, such as setting up a Fact-Checking Unit and partnering with social media platforms to flag false information. However, the responsibility to verify information lies with individual users as well. It's crucial to verify the authenticity of news before sharing it with others.

Additionally, cyberbullying is another major issue that needs to be addressed. With the anonymity offered by social media, people can easily hide behind their screens and harass others. This can have devastating consequences on the mental health of the victims. The Indian government has introduced stricter laws to tackle cyberbullying, and social media platforms have also stepped up their efforts to monitor and remove abusive content. However, it's essential for users to be mindful of their online behavior and to report any instances of bullying.

Privacy concerns are another major issue that needs to be addressed. With the amount of personal data shared online, there is a risk of this information falling into the wrong hands. The Indian government has introduced stricter data privacy regulations, such as the Personal Data Protection Bill, which aims to safeguard the privacy of individuals. Social media platforms have also introduced measures to protect user data, such as end-to-end encryption and two-factor authentication.

However, it's essential for users to be aware of the data they share and to take necessary precautions to protect their privacy.

In conclusion, social media has become an integral part of India's digital landscape, but it comes with its set of challenges. The government and social media platforms have introduced several measures to tackle these issues, but it's also crucial for individual users to be mindful of their behavior online. As social media continues to evolve, it's essential to adapt to the changing needs and preferences of users and harness its power to create new opportunities and drive positive change.

Strategies for Leveraging Social Media Platforms

1. Define your objectives and target audience

Before leveraging social media platforms, it is essential to define your objectives and target audience clearly. Are you looking to increase brand awareness, drive website traffic, generate leads, or improve customer engagement? Having a clear understanding of your goals will help you develop a focused social media strategy. Additionally, identify your target audience based on factors such as age, gender, location, interests, and online behavior. This information will guide you in choosing the right platforms and creating content that resonates with your audience.

One such example is the Indian e-commerce company Flipkart. They leveraged social media platforms to define their objectives and target audience to scale their business. Flipkart realized that social media is a powerful tool to reach its target audience, primarily young adults who are tech-savvy and frequently use social media platforms. They defined their objectives to increase brand awareness, drive website traffic, and boost sales.

To achieve these objectives, Flipkart developed targeted social media campaigns that were tailored to their audience's interests and behaviors. For example, they created videos featuring popular social media influencers and promoted them on platforms like Facebook, Instagram, and YouTube to increase brand awareness and drive website traffic.

Additionally, Flipkart leveraged social media platforms to create targeted ad campaigns, including retargeting ads and lookalike audiences, to boost sales and revenue. Flipkart offers a wide range of products on its platform, including electronics, fashion, home and kitchen appliances, furniture, books, beauty products, and more. By defining its objectives and target audience on social media platforms, Flipkart was able to successfully scale its business and become one of the leading e-commerce companies in India.

2. Choose the right platforms

Each social media platform has its unique characteristics and user demographics. Therefore, it is crucial to select the platforms that align with your target audience and objectives. For example, Instagram is ideal for visually appealing content targeting a younger audience, while LinkedIn is more suited for professional networking and B2B marketing. Research each platform's user demographics and features to make an informed decision.

One example of choosing the right platform for social media marketing is the Indian fashion brand, Myntra. Myntra leveraged Instagram's visual focus and popularity among its target audience of young, fashion-conscious consumers. The brand utilized Instagram Stories and Reels to showcase its products, collaborate with influencers, and create engaging content that resonated with its audience. By focusing on the platform that was most relevant to its target audience, Myntra was able to drive significant engagement and sales through its social media marketing efforts.

3. Create engaging content

Content is king in the realm of social media. To effectively leverage social media platforms, create high-quality, engaging, and relevant content that appeals to your target audience. Use a mix of content formats such as images, videos, articles, and polls to keep your audience engaged. Additionally, maintain a consistent brand voice and visual identity across all your social media channels.

An excellent example of this approach is Cadbury India's "Celebration of Love" campaign in 2019. The campaign featured a heartwarming video of an elderly couple exchanging Cadbury chocolates on the occasion of their anniversary, with the message of celebrating love and togetherness. The brand encouraged consumers to share their own stories of love on social media using the hashtag #SayItWithCadbury. The campaign garnered a lot of engagement and emotional responses from the audience, showcasing the power of storytelling and emotional appeal in creating engaging content.

4. Utilize hashtags and keywords

Hashtags and keywords play a vital role in increasing the visibility of your content on social media platforms. Research and use relevant hashtags and keywords related to your niche to improve your content's discoverability. Avoid overusing hashtags, as they may dilute your message and make it appear spammy.

One example of a company that utilized hashtags and keywords to increase engagement and reach on social media is Pepsi India. In 2019, they launched a campaign called #HarGhoontMeinSwag, which translates to "swag in every sip." The campaign encouraged users to share their unique swag moments with the hashtag #HarGhoontMeinSwag on social media. Pepsi India also used popular keywords and hashtags related to music, sports, and entertainment to target their audience and increase visibility. As a result, the campaign received over 400 million impressions on social media and helped increase brand awareness and engagement.

5. Engage with your audience

Social media is all about engagement and building relationships. Respond to comments, messages, and mentions promptly and genuinely. Ask questions, conduct polls, and encourage user-generated content to foster a sense of community and keep your audience engaged. By actively engaging with your audience, you can build strong connections and foster brand loyalty.

Durex, a leading brand in the condom market, is known for its witty and creative social media campaigns that stay up-to-date with the latest trends and platform updates. They leverage social media platforms to engage with their audience and promote sexual health in a fun and engaging way.

One of Durex's most successful campaigns was the #DontFakeIt campaign, which was aimed at raising awareness about the importance of using condoms. The campaign used a humorous approach to encourage safe sex practices and went viral on social media platforms like Twitter, Facebook, and Instagram.

In another campaign, Durex leveraged the trend of virtual reality and created a VR experience to educate people about condom usage. The campaign, called "Durex Explore," was launched on Facebook and was highly successful in generating engagement and awareness about sexual health.

Durex has also utilized the trend of influencer marketing to promote its brand. They collaborated with popular YouTubers and social media influencers to create entertaining and educational content about sexual health and safe sex practices.

In addition to staying up-to-date with social media trends and platform updates, Durex also utilizes data-driven decision-making in its social media campaigns. They analyze social media metrics and user engagement data to optimize their campaigns and improve their ROI. Overall, Durex's creative and innovative use of social media has helped them to stay relevant and engage with their audience on a deeper level while also promoting important messages about sexual health and safe sex practices.

6. Leverage influencers and partnerships

Influencer marketing and partnerships can significantly boost your social media presence. Collaborate with influencers who share your target audience and brand values to promote your products or services. Influencer endorsements can help you reach a wider audience and establish credibility. Similarly, partnering with other brands or organizations for joint campaigns or events can amplify your reach and generate positive brand associations.

Myntra Fashion Upgrade was a unique and innovative campaign launched by Myntra, one of India's largest online fashion retailers. The campaign aimed to encourage customers to recycle their old and unused clothes and get rewarded with discounts on new clothes. The campaign was launched in partnership with Goonj, an Indian non-governmental organization (NGO) working for the betterment of underprivileged communities. Myntra invited customers to donate their old clothes, which were then collected by Goonj and distributed to people in need.

To participate in the campaign, customers had to register on the Myntra app and select the "Fashion Upgrade" option. They could then choose to donate clothes by scheduling a pickup or dropping them off at a nearby Myntra store. In return, they received a Myntra Fashion Upgrade coupon, which offered them discounts on their next purchase. The campaign was a massive success, with thousands of customers participating and contributing to the cause. Myntra's partnership with Goonj not only helped them to drive sales but also allowed them to give back to the community and make a positive impact on society.

The campaign also helped Myntra to establish itself as a socially responsible and eco-friendly brand, which resonated well with its target audience. The success of the Myntra Fashion Upgrade campaign inspired other brands in India to launch similar initiatives, demonstrating the power of social media and partnerships in driving positive change.

Swiggy, an online food ordering and delivery platform in India, launched the "Swiggy Foodies" campaign to leverage the power of social media influencers and user-generated content to promote their brand. The campaign invited users to share their food pictures and reviews using the hashtag #SwiggyFoodies on social media platforms like Instagram, Twitter, and Facebook. The platform also collaborated with popular food bloggers and social media influencers who shared their Swiggy food experiences with their followers.

The campaign aimed to create a community of food enthusiasts and build brand awareness by encouraging user-generated content and influencer marketing. It also helped Swiggy to gain insights into user preferences and improve its offerings based on customer feedback. The campaign was a huge success, with thousands of users sharing their Swiggy food experiences and reviews on social media platforms. The hashtag #SwiggyFoodies became a trending topic on Twitter, with users sharing their food pictures and experiences. The platform also collaborated with several popular food bloggers and social media influencers, who shared their Swiggy food experiences with their followers, further increasing brand awareness.

Overall, the Swiggy Foodies campaign was a great example of how social media influencers and user-generated content can be leveraged to build brand awareness and create a community of loyal customers. It also showcased the importance of customer feedback and insights in improving product offerings and building customer loyalty.

Zomato, the popular online food ordering and delivery platform, launched an innovative social media campaign called "Zomato Premier League" during the 2018 Indian Premier League (IPL) season. The campaign was based on the idea of combining two of India's biggest passions - food and cricket. Zomato invited its users to predict the outcome of IPL matches, and in return, they could win prizes such as discounts, cashback, and other rewards.

To participate in the campaign, users had to log in to their Zomato account and predict the winner of each IPL match. They would earn points for each correct prediction and could climb the leaderboard to win bigger rewards. The campaign was a massive success, with thousands of users participating and engaging with Zomato on social media platforms. It helped the company increase its brand visibility and attract new users while also retaining its existing customer base.

By leveraging the popularity of IPL and combining it with its food delivery services, Zomato was able to create a unique and engaging social media campaign that resonated with its target audience. The success of the campaign also highlighted the power of social media in driving customer engagement and brand loyalty.

John Jacobs X Lenskart is a partnership campaign between two leading eyewear brands in India, John Jacobs and Lenskart. The campaign was launched in 2017 and was aimed at targeting the young and fashion-conscious audience in India who are looking for stylish and affordable eyewear.

The campaign leveraged the power of social media and influencer marketing to reach out to its target audience. They collaborated with several popular social media influencers and bloggers to create content around the campaign, including unboxing videos, product reviews, and style tips.

The campaign also included several online and offline initiatives, including pop-up stores, special discount offers, and experiential events. One of the highlights of the campaign was the launch of a limited edition collection of eyewear that was co-designed by John Jacobs and Lenskart.

The collaboration between John Jacobs and Lenskart proved to be a huge success, with the campaign generating significant buzz on social media and attracting a large number of customers. The campaign also helped to strengthen the position of both brands in the highly competitive Indian eyewear market.

The success of the John Jacobs X Lenskart campaign highlights the importance of partnerships and collaborations in the world of social media marketing. By joining forces and leveraging each other's strengths, brands can create campaigns that resonate with their target audience and drive significant growth and engagement.

MyIndiaMyTrips is a social media campaign launched by MakeMyTrip, one of the leading online travel companies in India. The campaign aimed to showcase the diverse culture, traditions, and natural beauty of India through the eyes of everyday travelers.

The campaign encouraged people to share their travel experiences on social media platforms such as Facebook, Twitter, and Instagram using the hashtag #MyIndiaMyTrips. The company then curated the best stories and photos and shared them on its social media channels, giving travelers a platform to share their experiences and inspire others to explore India.

MakeMyTrip partnered with several prominent influencers and bloggers, including travel photographer Ajay Sood and travel writer Shivya Nath, to reach a wider audience and encourage more people to participate in the campaign. The influencers shared their own travel stories and experiences through social media, further promoting the campaign and encouraging people to share their own stories.

The campaign was a huge success, generating over 20,000 user-generated content posts on social media platforms within a few months of its launch. The company saw a significant increase in engagement on its social media channels, with the campaign receiving over 2 million impressions and reaching more than 1.5 million people. Overall, the MyIndiaMyTrips campaign proved to be a great example of how social media can be leveraged to promote tourism and showcase the diverse cultural heritage of India through the eyes of everyday travelers.

7. Monitor and analyze the performance

Strategies for Leveraging Social Media Platforms

Monitor and Analyze Performance

One of the key aspects of a successful social media strategy is the continuous monitoring and analysis of your performance. Every post you make, every ad you run, every engagement you receive, contributes to a wealth of data that can provide invaluable insights into what's working and what's not.

Why It's Important

Monitoring and analyzing your social media performance enables you to understand the impact of your marketing efforts, identify trends, and make data-driven decisions. This, in turn, can lead to more effective strategies, higher engagement, and better return on investment (ROI).

Here are some ways to effectively monitor and analyze your social media performance:

1. Set Clear Goals

Firstly, define what success looks like for your business on social media. Are you looking to increase brand awareness, drive traffic to your website, generate leads, or drive sales? Setting clear, measurable goals is the first step in any performance monitoring and analysis strategy.

2. Use Social Media Analytics

Most social media platforms provide analytics tools that can help you track a variety of metrics. For instance, you can monitor reach, impressions, engagement rates, click-through rates, and conversion rates. Analyze these metrics in relation to your goals to assess the effectiveness of your strategies.

3. Leverage Third-Party Tools

There are numerous third-party tools available that can provide deeper insights into your social media performance. Tools like Hootsuite, Buffer, and Sprout Social can help you track metrics across multiple platforms, monitor mentions of your brand, analyze sentiment, and much more.

4. Regularly Review and Adjust Your Strategy

Social media is constantly evolving, and what worked yesterday might not work tomorrow. Regularly review your performance, and don't be afraid to adjust your strategy based on your findings.

8. Utilize paid advertising

Organic reach can be limited on social media platforms due to algorithm changes and high competition. To expand your reach, consider utilizing paid advertising options such as Facebook Ads, Instagram Ads, LinkedIn Sponsored Content, or Twitter Ads. With precise targeting capabilities, paid advertising can help you reach a larger and more relevant audience, ultimately driving better results.

Examples of companies that effectively used paid advertising to boost their visibility and achieve their goals include:

1. OYO Rooms: OYO Rooms, a leading Indian hospitality chain, revolutionized the budget hotel space in India. To scale their business, they utilized paid advertising on Facebook. By targeting specific audience demographics like young professionals and frequent travelers, they showcased their affordable and comfortable accommodations. Utilizing Facebook's retargeting capabilities, they reached out to people who had visited their website but had not yet booked a room. The paid advertising strategy allowed OYO Rooms to reach a wider audience and increase their bookings.

2. Big Basket: Big Basket, India's largest online grocery store, aimed to expand its customer base. They leveraged paid search advertising

on Google, targeting keywords like "online grocery store," "fresh produce delivery," and "pantry essentials" to reach people actively searching for their products. Google's remarketing capabilities were also employed to show ads to previous website visitors who had not made a purchase. The paid search advertising strategy successfully drove more traffic to their website and increased their sales.

3. UrbanClap: UrbanClap, a prominent online marketplace for local services in India, used paid advertising on social media platforms such as Facebook and Instagram to enhance visibility and attract new customers. They targeted specific audience demographics based on location, age, and interests while showcasing their range of services and competitive pricing. Employing social media's retargeting capabilities, they reached out to people who had previously visited their website but had not yet booked a service. The paid advertising on social media helped UrbanClap reach a wider audience and increase their bookings.

4. Byju's: Byju's, India's largest ed-tech company, provides online courses and study materials for students of all ages. To reach more students and parents, Byju utilized paid advertising on YouTube. Engaging video ads were created to showcase their courses and teaching methods, with targeting based on specific audience demographics like age and education level. Leveraging YouTube's advertising capabilities, Byju's reached a wider audience and increased their enrollments.

5. MakeMyTrip: MakeMyTrip, India's leading online travel company, offers a wide range of travel services, including flights, hotels,

and vacation packages. To boost bookings, MakeMyTrip utilized paid advertising on Google AdWords. They targeted specific travel and tourism keywords and created engaging ads highlighting their competitive pricing and services. Additionally, AdWords' remarketing capabilities were used to show ads to people who had visited their website but had not yet booked a trip. By leveraging paid advertising on AdWords, MakeMyTrip expanded its reach and increased its bookings.

9. Stay up-to-date with trends and platform updates: Social media platforms are constantly evolving, with new features and trends emerging regularly. To stay competitive, keep yourself updated with the latest trends, platform updates, and best practices. Participate in industry events, follow relevant blogs and thought leaders, and join online communities to stay informed and adapt your strategies accordingly.

10. Experiment and iterate: Finally, don't be afraid to experiment with different content formats, posting times, and strategies. Social media is an ever-changing landscape, and what works today might not work tomorrow. Regularly test new ideas, analyze the results, and iterate your strategies to stay ahead of the competition and maximize your social media success.

Real-time examples

1. Zomato, an Indian food delivery service, has successfully leveraged social media platforms to create engaging content and interact with its audience. They use a mix of witty, relatable memes, user-generated content, and timely promotions to keep their followers entertained and informed. By using humor and

staying up-to-date with current events, Zomato has built a strong social media presence, resulting in increased brand awareness and customer loyalty.

2. Nykaa, an Indian beauty and wellness e-commerce platform, has utilized social media to create a strong community around its brand. They collaborate with influencers, host giveaways, and share user-generated content, all of which help them build trust and engage their target audience. Moreover, Nykaa actively engages with its followers by responding to comments and messages, making the brand more accessible and personable.

3. OnePlus, a smartphone manufacturer, has effectively used social media platforms to create buzz around its product launches and engage with its tech-savvy audience. They regularly share product teasers, behind-the-scenes content, and customer testimonials to generate excitement and anticipation. Additionally, OnePlus utilizes social media to provide customer support, answer queries, and resolve issues, showcasing their commitment to customer satisfaction.

4. Chumbak, an Indian lifestyle brand known for its quirky designs, has harnessed the power of social media platforms to create visually appealing content that resonates with its target audience. Their Instagram feed is a perfect example of consistent visual identity and a well-curated collection of colorful images showcasing their products. Chumbak also encourages user-generated content by featuring customers' photos and stories, fostering a sense of community and brand loyalty.

5. Swiggy, another Indian food delivery service, has used social media to create relatable content that highlights the convenience and variety offered by its platform. They often use humor, trending topics, and creative visuals to engage with their audience and reinforce their brand identity. Swiggy also leverages paid advertising on social media platforms to expand its reach and target potential customers effectively.

By learning from these real-time examples and implementing the strategies outlined above, businesses can successfully leverage social media platforms to achieve their marketing objectives and foster meaningful connections with their audience.

Case Study 1: Amul - The Taste of India

Amul is a leading dairy cooperative in India, known for its butter, milk, cheese, and other dairy products. Over the years, Amul has consistently used social media to build a strong brand presence and engage with its audience.

One of their most successful social media campaigns is the "Amul Topical," a series of creative and witty illustrations that comment on current events and popular culture. These illustrations, which often feature Amul's mascot, "The Utterly Butterly Girl," are shared across Facebook, Twitter, and Instagram, garnering a lot of attention and engagement from their followers.

The success of Amul Topical can be attributed to the following factors:

1. Timeliness: Amul's social media team quickly responds to current events and trending topics, creating illustrations that are relevant and shareable.

2. Creativity: The illustrations are unique, visually appealing, and often humorous, making them highly shareable and engaging.

3. Brand consistency: Amul has maintained a consistent visual style and tone in its illustrations, reinforcing its brand identity and making its content easily recognizable.

4. Emotional appeal: By touching upon topics that resonate with their audience, Amul's social media content evokes a sense of nostalgia and affinity towards the brand.

Case Study 2: Vodafone India - ZooZoos

Vodafone India, a leading telecommunications service provider, launched the iconic "ZooZoos" campaign during the 2009 Indian Premier League (IPL). The ZooZoos are cute, egg-headed characters that were featured in a series of short and humorous ads promoting Vodafone's various products and services.

The ZooZoos campaign went viral on social media, especially on Facebook and Twitter, where Vodafone India actively engaged with their audience by sharing exclusive content, conducting contests, and hosting live chats.

The success of the ZooZoos campaign can be attributed to the following factors:

1. Emotional appeal: The ZooZoos characters were unique, endearing, and memorable, capturing the hearts of millions of viewers and creating a strong emotional connection with the brand.

2. Consistency: The campaign was well-planned and executed over an extended period, with new ads and content being released throughout the IPL season, keeping the audience engaged and looking forward to more.

3. Integration with traditional media: The ZooZoos campaign seamlessly integrated television ads with social media, using both platforms to amplify the campaign's reach and impact.

4. Audience Engagement: Vodafone India actively engaged with their audience on social media platforms, creating a sense of community and brand loyalty.

Case Study 3: MakeMyTrip - #GreatIndianGetaway

MakeMyTrip, a leading online travel company in India, launched the #GreatIndianGetaway campaign in 2016 with the objective of promoting domestic tourism and encouraging Indians to explore their own country.

The campaign featured a series of short videos showcasing various destinations in India, accompanied by a contest where participants could win exciting travel vouchers. These videos were shared across Facebook, Twitter, Instagram, and YouTube, generating a significant amount of engagement and buzz around the campaign.

The success of the #GreatIndianGetaway campaign can be attributed to the following factors:

1. Storytelling: The videos featured relatable and inspiring stories of travelers exploring India, making them appealing and engaging to a wide audience.

2. Visual appeal: The campaign's videos were beautifully shot and visually stunning, showcasing the diversity and beauty of India's landscape and culture.

3. User-generated content: MakeMyTrip encouraged their audience to share their own travel stories and experiences using the campaign hashtag, generating additional buzz and engagement around the campaign.

4. Incentives: The contest element of the campaign added excitement and motivation for the audience to participate and share their own stories, increasing the campaign's reach and impact.

Case Study 4: Swiggy - #WhatTheFalooda

Swiggy, a popular online food delivery service in India, launched the #WhatTheFalooda campaign in 2018 to address a common pain point for their customers - late deliveries. The campaign aimed to create awareness about Swiggy's promise to compensate customers for late deliveries while also generating some fun and humor around the topic.

The campaign featured a series of witty and humorous social media posts, GIFs, and short videos, shared across Facebook, Twitter, and Instagram. The content focused on the idea that when a delivery is late, customers might say, "What is the Falooda?" (a play on words using a popular Indian dessert). The campaign garnered a lot of engagement, with customers sharing their own late delivery experiences and appreciating Swiggy's transparency and accountability.

The success of the #WhatTheFalooda campaign can be attributed to the following factors:

1. Relatability: The campaign addressed a genuine pain point for customers, making it highly relatable and engaging.

2. Humor: Swiggy used humor to address a potentially negative topic, making the campaign enjoyable and shareable.

3. Brand personality: The campaign showcased Swiggy's fun and quirky brand personality, helping to differentiate the brand from its competitors.

4. Transparency and accountability: By addressing the issue of late deliveries and promising compensation, Swiggy demonstrated its commitment to customer satisfaction, building trust and loyalty among its customers.

These case studies demonstrate the power of social media in amplifying marketing campaigns and engaging with audiences in India. The successful campaigns share common elements such as relatability, creativity, emotional appeal, and audience engagement. By understanding and applying these strategies, businesses can leverage social media platforms to create impactful campaigns that resonate with their target audience and drive brand growth.

6

Innovating Marketing Strategies

Introduction As the business landscape evolves, marketing strategies must adapt to keep up with changing customer behavior, technological advancements, and market dynamics. In this subsection, we will compare traditional marketing techniques with new trends and explore how businesses can innovate their marketing strategies to stay competitive in today's fast-paced world.

Traditional Marketing

Traditional marketing includes print advertising, billboards, television and radio commercials, direct mail, and telemarketing. These techniques have been used for decades to reach potential customers, build brand awareness, and drive sales. While traditional marketing can still be effective in specific contexts, it has several limitations:

1. Limited targeting: Traditional marketing methods often cannot target specific demographics, leading to wasted resources and missed opportunities.

2. High costs: Traditional marketing can be expensive, especially for smaller businesses with limited budgets.

3. Difficulty measuring ROI: It can be challenging to accurately measure the return on investment (ROI) of traditional marketing campaigns, making it difficult to determine their effectiveness.

4. One-way communication: Traditional marketing methods are generally passive and one-way, offering limited opportunities for interaction and engagement with customers.

New Trends in Marketing

In contrast to traditional marketing, new trends in marketing focus on leveraging digital technologies, data-driven insights, and innovative techniques to reach and engage customers. Some of the key trends include:

1. Digital marketing: Digital marketing encompasses various online marketing channels, such as search engine optimization (SEO), pay-per-click advertising (PPC), email marketing, content marketing, and social media marketing. These methods offer numerous advantages over traditional marketing, such as precise targeting, real-time analytics, lower costs, and the ability to interact with customers directly.

2. Mobile marketing: As smartphone usage continues to rise, mobile marketing has become a crucial component of modern marketing strategies. Mobile marketing includes tactics like app-based advertising, location-based marketing, SMS marketing, and mobile search ads. These methods enable businesses to reach customers on mobile devices, offering personalized and contextual experiences.

3. Influencer marketing: Involves partnering with influential individuals, often on social media platforms, to promote a brand or product. This type of marketing capitalizes on the trust and credibility that influencers have built with their followers, often resulting in higher engagement and conversion rates than traditional advertising.

4. Experiential marketing: Focuses on creating immersive, memorable customer experiences, often blending the physical and digital worlds. This can include tactics like pop-up events, virtual reality experiences, or interactive installations. Experiential marketing aims to generate buzz, foster emotional connections, and create lasting impressions that customers associate with a brand.

5. Data-driven marketing: Leverages big data and advanced analytics to gain insights into customer behavior, preferences, and trends. These insights can inform targeted, personalized marketing campaigns that are more likely to resonate with customers and drive results.

Innovating Marketing Strategies

Companies must continuously innovate their marketing strategies to stay competitive in today's rapidly changing business landscape. This can include:

1. Embracing digital technologies: Businesses should invest in digital marketing channels and tools that enable them to reach and engage customers more effectively, efficiently, and cost-effectively than traditional marketing methods.

2. Focusing on customer-centricity: By prioritizing customer needs, preferences, and behaviors, companies can develop targeted marketing campaigns that resonate with their audience and drive results.

3. Harnessing data and analytics: Companies should leverage data and analytics to gain insights into customer behavior and inform their marketing strategies, enabling them to make more informed decisions and optimize their campaigns for maximum impact.

4. Encouraging creativity and innovation: Companies should foster a culture that promotes creativity and innovation, allowing employees to experiment with new marketing tactics and approaches. This can lead to discovering unique and effective strategies that differentiate the brand and resonate with customers.

5. Integrating online and offline strategies: Businesses should strive to create a seamless experience for customers by integrating their online and offline marketing efforts. This can include combining

traditional advertising with digital channels, using technology to enhance in-store experiences, or developing omnichannel campaigns that reach customers across multiple touchpoints.

6. Personalization and customization: Personalized marketing efforts, such as tailored email campaigns or targeted social media ads, can help businesses stand out in a crowded marketplace and better engage their audience. By using data and analytics to understand customer preferences, companies can develop marketing messages that resonate with individual consumers.

7. Adopting an agile approach: Marketing teams should embrace an agile mindset, regularly reviewing and adjusting their strategies based on data and feedback. This iterative approach allows businesses to respond quickly to changing market conditions and customer preferences, ensuring their marketing efforts remain relevant and effective.

Real-Time Examples

1. Coca-Cola's 'Share a Coke' campaign: This innovative campaign replaced the company's logo on bottles with popular names, encouraging customers to find and share a Coke with their friends. The campaign seamlessly blended traditional packaging with digital marketing efforts, such as personalized online ads and social media engagement, resulting in increased sales and brand exposure.

2. Nike's 'Nike Run Club' app: Nike leveraged mobile marketing and gamification to create a popular fitness app that engages users with personalized coaching, fitness challenges, and social

features. The app helps build brand loyalty and drive sales by encouraging users to purchase Nike products and participate in branded events.

3. Starbucks' mobile app and rewards program: Starbucks integrated mobile marketing and loyalty program strategies to create a seamless customer experience both in-store and online. The app allows customers to order and pay for their drinks, accumulate rewards points, and receive personalized offers and discounts, driving customer engagement and repeat business.

4. Dove's 'Real Beauty Sketches' campaign: This social media campaign leveraged influencer marketing and emotional storytelling to challenge societal beauty standards and promote Dove's brand values. The campaign's powerful message resonated with consumers, garnering millions of views on YouTube and widespread media coverage.

By embracing new trends in marketing and continuously innovating their strategies, businesses can better engage their target audience, differentiate themselves from competitors, and drive long-term growth and success.

Integrating Technology into Marketing Efforts

The rapid evolution of technology has transformed the way businesses market their products and services. Today, companies must leverage cutting-edge tools and platforms to create more targeted, personalized, and engaging marketing campaigns. In this section, we'll explore various ways in which businesses can integrate technology into their marketing efforts to drive success.

1. **Data-driven decision-making**

Modern marketing relies heavily on data to make informed decisions. By analyzing customer data, businesses can better understand their target audience, identify trends, and develop more effective marketing strategies. Key data-driven technologies include:

- Customer Relationship Management (CRM) systems, allow businesses to collect, store, and analyze customer information, such as purchase history and demographics.

- Web analytics tools, such as Google Analytics, track user behavior on websites and provide insights into user preferences and engagement.

- Social media analytics tools that analyze user interactions and sentiment on social platforms to inform content strategies and identify potential influencers.

2. **Artificial intelligence and machine learning**

Artificial intelligence (AI) and machine learning (ML) technologies are increasingly being used in marketing to automate tasks, predict customer behavior, and optimize campaigns. Some applications of AI and ML in marketing include:

- Chatbots and virtual assistants can automate customer support and provide personalized product recommendations based on customer preferences.

- Predictive analytics uses ML algorithms to analyze customer data and predict future behavior, such as the likelihood of a purchase or the potential for churn.

- AI-powered content generation tools that can create personalized emails, social media posts, and other marketing materials based on customer data and preferences.

3. Augmented and virtual reality

Augmented reality (AR) and virtual reality (VR) technologies offer new ways for businesses to engage customers and provide immersive experiences. These technologies can be used in marketing to:

- Create interactive product demonstrations or virtual showrooms that allow customers to explore products and features in a more engaging way.

- Develop immersive brand experiences or virtual events that provide unique opportunities for customer interaction and engagement.

- Enhance traditional marketing materials, such as print ads or product packaging, with AR elements that add a digital layer of interactivity.

An Indian company that has effectively integrated augmented reality (AR) and virtual reality (VR) into its marketing efforts is Lenskart, a leading eyewear retailer. Founded in 2010 by Peyush Bansal, Amit Chaudhary, and Sumeet Kapahi, Lenskart has revolutionized the way consumers shop for eyewear by leveraging innovative technologies like AR and VR.

One of Lenskart's most notable innovations is its 3D Try-On feature, which uses AR technology to enable customers to virtually try on different eyewear styles using their smartphones or computer cameras. By superimposing the selected glasses onto the user's face in real time, the 3D Try-On feature allows customers to see how various frames look on them, making the online shopping experience more interactive and engaging.

In addition to the 3D Try-On feature, Lenskart has also experimented with VR technology to provide immersive in-store experiences for customers. For instance, the company has set up virtual reality booths in some of its physical stores, where customers can put on a VR headset and explore a virtual store environment. This allows them to browse through Lenskart's vast collection of eyewear and virtually try on different styles, further enhancing the shopping experience.

Lenskart's use of AR and VR technology has not only improved customer satisfaction and engagement but has also provided the company with valuable data on customer preferences and behavior. By analyzing this data, Lenskart can better understand its customers' needs, optimize its product offerings, and tailor its marketing strategies accordingly.

By integrating AR and VR into its marketing efforts, Lenskart has successfully created a seamless and enjoyable shopping experience for its customers, setting it apart from traditional eyewear retailers and contributing to its rapid growth and success in the Indian market.

4. Mobile Marketing

With the widespread adoption of smartphones and mobile devices, businesses must prioritize mobile marketing to reach customers where they spend a significant amount of their time. Key mobile marketing strategies include:

- Mobile-optimized websites and landing pages, which ensure that content is easily accessible and navigable on mobile devices.

- Mobile apps can provide personalized experiences, loyalty programs, and in-app marketing opportunities.

- Location-based marketing, which uses geolocation data to deliver targeted ads and offers to customers based on their physical location.

Another Indian company that has effectively leveraged mobile marketing to reach its audience and scale its operations is Paytm, a leading digital payments and financial services platform. Founded in 2010 by Vijay Shekhar Sharma, Paytm has become one of the largest mobile payment platforms in India, with millions of users and merchants.

Paytm recognized the potential of mobile marketing in driving user acquisition and engagement, given the increasing adoption of smartphones and mobile internet in India. They developed a user-friendly mobile app for Android and iOS platforms, which allows users to make payments, recharge mobiles and DTH, book tickets, and access various financial services.

To drive app downloads and user engagement, Paytm has employed various mobile marketing strategies, including:

1. App Store optimization (ASO): Paytm focused on optimizing its app listing on the Google Play Store and Apple App Store,

using relevant keywords, engaging app icons, screenshots, and descriptions to improve visibility and encourage downloads.

2. Mobile Advertising: Paytm has run targeted mobile ad campaigns on various platforms, such as social media, ad networks, and in-app advertising, to reach potential users and drive app installs.

3. Referral programs: Paytm introduced a referral program that rewards both the referrer and the new user with cashback or discount coupons, encouraging users to share the app with friends and family.

4. Push notifications and in-app messaging: Paytm leverages push notifications and in-app messaging to keep users engaged, sending personalized offers, reminders, and updates to drive transactions.

5. Partnerships and integrations: Paytm has partnered with several businesses and services, allowing users to make payments via the Paytm app, thus increasing its visibility and reach.

These mobile marketing strategies have helped Paytm expand its user base and establish itself as a leading player in the Indian digital payments market.

5. Marketing automation

Marketing automation platforms help businesses streamline and automate various marketing tasks, such as email campaigns, social media posting, and lead nurturing. By automating repetitive tasks, businesses can save time and resources while ensuring consistent and timely marketing efforts. Key features of marketing automation platforms include:

- Automated email marketing, which allows businesses to create and send personalized email campaigns based on customer behavior and preferences.

- Lead scoring and nurturing, which uses customer data to identify and prioritize high-value leads and deliver targeted marketing content.

- Social media scheduling and management tools that automate the process of posting and engaging with users on social platforms.

An example of a company that has effectively used marketing automation to scale its business in India is Freshworks, a Software as a Service (SaaS) company providing customer engagement and business software solutions. Founded by Girish Mathrubootham and Shan Krishnasamy in 2010, Freshworks has grown into a global company with a vast customer base.

Freshworks has leveraged marketing automation to streamline its marketing efforts, improve lead generation, and enhance customer relationship management. The company uses its suite of products, including Freshmarketer, to implement marketing automation strategies. Some of these strategies include:

1. Lead scoring and segmentation: Freshworks uses marketing automation tools to score leads based on their behavior and interaction with the company's digital assets. This allows the company to segment leads based on their interests, engagement

levels, and readiness to purchase, resulting in more personalized and targeted marketing efforts.

2. Email marketing campaigns: Freshworks automates its email marketing campaigns, sending personalized and timely emails to its leads and customers based on their actions, preferences, and stage in the sales funnel. This helps improve engagement and drive conversions.

3. Drip marketing campaigns: Freshworks employs drip marketing campaigns to nurture leads over time, sending relevant content and offers to prospects at regular intervals. Marketing automation allows Freshworks to create, schedule, and manage these campaigns more efficiently.

4. Conversion rate optimization (CRO): Freshworks uses marketing automation tools to track user behavior on its website and landing pages. These insights help the company identify areas for improvement and optimize its online presence to drive better conversion rates.

5. Analytics and reporting: Marketing automation provides Freshworks with valuable data and insights into its marketing campaigns' performance. The company can easily track key metrics, such as click-through rates, conversions, and return on investment, helping it make data-driven decisions and optimize its marketing efforts.

By integrating marketing automation into its operations, Freshworks has managed to improve the efficiency of its marketing processes, increase lead generation, and enhance customer relationships, contributing to the company's impressive growth.

6. Video Marketing

Video content is an increasingly important aspect of modern marketing, offering businesses a powerful medium for storytelling and customer engagement. By leveraging video marketing tools and platforms, businesses can:

Another example of a company that has successfully used video marketing in India is Swiggy, an online food delivery platform. Founded in 2014, Swiggy has rapidly expanded its presence across India, connecting consumers with their favorite restaurants and food outlets.

Swiggy has effectively leveraged video marketing to promote its services, create brand awareness, and engage its target audience. Some key aspects of Swiggy's video marketing strategy include:

1. Humorous content: Swiggy creates funny and relatable videos that resonate with its audience. These videos often depict everyday situations and showcase how Swiggy's services can simplify people's lives. The humor helps to make the videos shareable, which leads to increased brand exposure.

2. Influencer partnerships: Swiggy collaborates with popular influencers and content creators to produce engaging videos that showcase its services. These influencers help Swiggy reach a larger audience and enhance its brand image.

3. Seasonal and event-based campaigns: Swiggy creates video campaigns around popular events, festivals, and seasonal themes. For example, during cricket tournaments, Swiggy has launched video campaigns that promote special offers and discounts to attract more customers.

4. Advertisements: Swiggy has also invested in video advertisements that are broadcast on television and digital platforms. These ads use a mix of humor, emotion, and storytelling to communicate the brand's message and promote its services.

By using video marketing effectively, Swiggy has been able to establish itself as a leading food delivery platform in India, attracting millions of users and driving significant growth.

In conclusion, integrating technology into marketing efforts is essential for businesses to stay competitive and connect with their target audiences in today's fast-paced digital landscape. By leveraging data-driven decision-making, AI and ML, AR and VR, mobile marketing, marketing automation, and video marketing, companies can create more personalized, engaging, and effective marketing campaigns.

Adopting these technologies requires businesses to be flexible and open to change, as well as to invest in the necessary tools, platforms, and employee training. However, the benefits of technological integration in marketing far outweigh the costs, as businesses can gain valuable insights into customer behavior, streamline marketing processes, and ultimately increase their reach and conversion rates.

By staying up-to-date with the latest marketing trends and technologies, businesses can ensure that they continue to innovate and adapt to the ever-changing needs and expectations of their customers, leading to long-term success in the increasingly competitive Indian market.

What is Performance Marketing?

Introduction

Performance marketing has revolutionized the world of digital advertising, enabling businesses to track, measure, and optimize their marketing efforts based on quantifiable metrics. This data-driven approach ensures that marketers can make informed decisions and allocate their resources effectively, thereby maximizing their return on ad spend (ROAS) and achieving their business goals.

This chapter delves into the intricacies of performance marketing, providing an overview of its key components, strategies, and tools, as well as real-life examples and case studies that showcase its potential. It also offers insights into measuring ROAS and other essential performance metrics to ensure optimal results.

1. Understanding Performance Marketing

Performance marketing is an advertising model that focuses on measurable outcomes, such as leads, sales, or app installs, rather than traditional metrics, like impressions or clicks. Marketers only pay for the desired results, which reduces wastage and ensures a higher ROI. Some common performance marketing channels include:

- Affiliate Marketing
- Pay-Per-Click (PPC) Advertising
- Search Engine Marketing (SEM)

- Social Media Advertising

- Native Advertising

- Email Marketing

- Influencer Marketing

2. **Key Terminologies in Performance Marketing**

- Return on Ad Spend (ROAS): A measure of the revenue generated for every dollar spent on advertising. It is calculated by dividing the revenue generated by the ad spend.

- Cost Per Action (CPA): The amount an advertiser pays for each specified action (e.g., sale, lead, or click) taken by a user.

- Conversion Rate (CVR): The percentage of users who complete a desired action (e.g., purchase) out of the total number of users who clicked on an ad.

- Click-Through Rate (CTR): The percentage of users who clicked on an ad out of the total number of users who saw the ad.

- Customer Acquisition Cost (CAC): The total cost of acquiring a new customer, including marketing and sales expenses.

- Customer Lifetime Value (CLV): The total net profit generated by a customer over their entire relationship with a company.

3. **Performance Marketing Strategies**

3.1. Choosing the Right Channels: Selecting the most suitable performance marketing channels depends on factors like the target audience, marketing goals, and budget. Experimenting with different channels and analyzing their performance can help identify the most effective ones.

3.2. Targeting and Segmentation: Creating detailed customer personas and using demographic, geographic, and behavioral data to segment audiences can improve targeting and boost conversion rates.

3.3. Personalization and Dynamic Content: Personalizing ad creatives and landing pages based on user behavior and preferences can enhance the user experience and increase conversions.

3.4. A/B Testing and Optimization: Regularly testing different ad creatives, headlines, CTAs, and landing pages can help identify the best-performing elements and improve campaign performance.

3.5. Data-Driven Decision Making: Using data and analytics to monitor, measure, and adjust marketing efforts can help optimize campaigns and maximize ROAS.

4. Measuring Performance Metrics

4.1. ROAS: Tracking ROAS allows marketers to evaluate the effectiveness of their advertising campaigns and allocate resources accordingly. To calculate ROAS, divide the total revenue generated by the total ad spend. For example, if a campaign generates $5,000 in revenue and costs $1,000, the ROAS is 5 ($5,000 / $1,000).

4.2. Other Metrics: Monitoring additional performance metrics like CPA, CVR, CTR, CAC, and CLV can provide valuable insights into campaign performance, customer behavior, and overall business health.

5. Tools and Platforms for Performance Marketing

There is a wide range of tools and platforms available to help marketers implement and manage their performance marketing campaigns effectively. Some of the most popular ones include:

5.1. Google Ads: A comprehensive platform for running search, display, and video ad campaigns on Google and its partner websites. It offers extensive targeting options, automated bidding strategies, and advanced analytics.

5.2. Facebook Ads Manager: A powerful tool for creating, managing, and tracking ad campaigns across Facebook, Instagram, Messenger, and the Audience Network. It provides granular audience targeting, dynamic creative optimization, and in-depth reporting.

5.3. Google Analytics: A widely used web analytics platform that helps marketers track user behavior, monitor campaign performance, and make data-driven decisions to optimize their marketing efforts.

5.4. HubSpot: An all-in-one inbound marketing, sales, and customer service platform that offers tools for email marketing, content creation, social media management, and marketing automation, among others.

5.5. Affiliate Networks: Platforms like Commission Junction, ShareASale, and Impact Radius connect advertisers with publishers and manage affiliate marketing campaigns, tracking, and payments.

New Trends in Performance Marketing

1. Artificial Intelligence and Machine Learning

One of the most significant trends in performance marketing is the adoption of artificial intelligence (AI) and machine learning.

These technologies enable marketers to analyze vast amounts of data, identify patterns, and make data-driven decisions to optimize campaigns. AI-powered tools can automate routine tasks, such as keyword research, ad bidding, and audience targeting, while machine learning algorithms continuously learn and adjust to optimize campaign performance.

2. Influencer Marketing

Influencer marketing has emerged as a powerful performance marketing strategy, leveraging the reach and credibility of social media influencers to promote products and services. By partnering with influencers who have a strong connection with their audience, businesses can achieve higher engagement rates and better results. This approach works particularly well for niche markets, where influencers have a deep understanding of their followers' preferences and can recommend products with authenticity.

3. Omnichannel Marketing

Omnichannel marketing is the integration of various marketing channels, such as email, social media, search, and display advertising, to create a seamless and consistent experience for customers. This approach ensures that businesses can reach their target audience across multiple touchpoints, improving the chances of conversion. It also allows marketers to collect and analyze data from different channels, enabling them to fine-tune their strategies and drive better results.

4. Personalization

As consumers become more sophisticated and expect personalized experiences, businesses need to tailor their marketing efforts accordingly. Personalization in performance marketing involves using data-driven insights to create customized messages and offers that resonate with individual customers. This approach can help improve conversion rates, customer satisfaction, and brand loyalty.

5. Video Advertising

With the growing popularity of video content on social media platforms, video advertising has become a crucial aspect of performance marketing. Businesses can leverage video ads to engage audiences, convey complex messages, and showcase products more effectively. Interactive video ads, which allow viewers to engage with the content, are particularly effective at driving conversions and boosting brand awareness.

How Small Businesses in India Can Utilize Performance Marketing

1. Target the Right Audience

For small businesses in India, identifying and targeting the right audience is crucial for the success of their performance marketing campaigns. By leveraging data and analytics tools, businesses can segment their audience based on factors such as demographics, interests, and online behavior. This will enable them to create tailored campaigns that resonate with their target audience and drive higher conversion rates.

2. Use Local Influencers

Small businesses in India can benefit from partnering with local influencers who have a strong connection with their community. These influencers can help promote the business's products and services to a highly engaged audience, increasing brand awareness and driving sales. Moreover, local influencers can provide valuable insights into the preferences and needs of the local market, enabling businesses to fine-tune their offerings and marketing strategies.

3. Leverage Social Media Platforms

Social media platforms, such as Facebook, Instagram, and Twitter, offer small businesses in India an affordable and effective way to reach their target audience. By creating engaging content and leveraging the platform's targeting capabilities, businesses can drive website traffic, generate leads, and increase sales. Additionally, social media platforms provide businesses with valuable insights into audience behavior and preferences, which can be used to optimize their marketing strategies.

4. Test and Optimize

Continuous testing and optimization are essential for small businesses in India to maximize the ROI of their performance marketing campaigns. By experimenting with different ad formats, messaging, and targeting options, businesses can identify what works best for their audience and refine their strategies accordingly. Analyzing campaign performance data, such as click-through rates, conversion rates, and return on ad spend, will enable businesses to make data-driven decisions and allocate resources more effectively.

Utilize Free and Low-Cost Tools

Many free and low-cost tools are available to help small businesses in India manage and optimize their performance marketing efforts. For example, Google Ads offers a range of tools for keyword research, campaign creation, and performance tracking. Similarly, Facebook Ads

Manager provides comprehensive targeting options and analytics to help businesses reach their ideal audience. By leveraging these tools, small businesses can execute performance marketing campaigns on a limited budget and achieve impressive results.

Collaborate with Other Local Businesses

Small businesses in India can amplify their performance marketing efforts by collaborating with other local businesses. This can involve cross-promotion, co-hosting events, or offering special deals and discounts to customers who shop at both establishments. Such collaborations can help businesses expand their reach, increase brand awareness, and create a strong local presence.

Prioritize Mobile Marketing

With the rapid growth of mobile usage in India, it's essential for small businesses to prioritize mobile marketing in their performance marketing strategies. This can include optimizing websites for mobile devices, creating mobile-friendly content, and using mobile-specific ad formats, such as in-app ads and mobile search ads. By focusing on mobile marketing, small businesses can reach a larger audience and drive higher engagement rates.

6. Case Studies: Successful Performance Marketing Campaigns in India

Case Study 1: Zomato

Zomato, an Indian online food delivery service, has implemented a variety of performance marketing strategies to expand its user base and increase order volume.

Targeted Ads: Zomato leveraged data-driven insights to create targeted ads for its audience. By analyzing user behavior, preferences, and demographics, Zomato developed personalized ad campaigns to attract new users and re-engage existing ones. The company used a mix of search, display, and social media ads to reach potential customers and drive app downloads.

Influencer Marketing: Zomato partnered with popular food bloggers and influencers to promote its services. These influencers shared their experiences with Zomato, creating authentic content that resonated with their followers. This strategy helped Zomato tap into a wider audience and increase brand awareness.

App Referral Program: To encourage existing users to refer their friends and family, Zomato launched a referral program. Users received discounts and rewards for each successful referral, which incentivized them to share the app with their network. This strategy helped Zomato acquire new users at a lower cost and boost its overall user base.

Case Study 2: Nykaa

Nykaa, an Indian e-commerce platform for beauty and wellness products, has successfully implemented performance marketing strategies to drive sales and growth.

Affiliate Marketing: Nykaa collaborated with various affiliates, such as beauty bloggers, influencers, and cashback websites, to promote its products. By offering affiliates a commission for each sale generated through their referral links, Nykaa created a cost-effective marketing channel that drove high-quality traffic and increased sales.

Retargeting Campaigns: Nykaa used retargeting ads to re-engage potential customers who had previously visited their website without making a purchase. These ads showcased personalized product recommendations based on user's browsing history, encouraging them to return to the website and complete their purchase.

Personalized Email Marketing: Nykaa leveraged customer data to create personalized email campaigns with tailored product recommendations, discounts, and offers. By segmenting its audience based on their preferences, purchase history, and online behavior, Nykaa sent relevant emails that resulted in higher open and click-through rates, ultimately driving sales.

Case Study 3: Paytm

Paytm, a leading Indian digital wallet and payment service, has utilized performance marketing to acquire new users and increase transaction volume.

Cashback Offers: Paytm implemented cashback offers as a core marketing strategy, providing users with incentives to use their services for various transactions, such as mobile recharges, bill payments, and online shopping. These offers helped Paytm attract new users and increase the frequency of transactions among existing ones.

Cross-Channel Marketing: Paytm adopted a cross-channel marketing approach, using a combination of search, display, and social media ads to reach its target audience. By leveraging data-driven insights, Paytm created tailored ad campaigns that resonated with users and drove app downloads and transactions.

Strategic Partnerships: Paytm forged partnerships with various merchants, e-commerce platforms, and service providers, offering its users exclusive discounts and offers when using Paytm for payments. These partnerships allowed Paytm to provide added value to its users while simultaneously increasing its transaction volume.

These case studies illustrate the effectiveness of performance marketing strategies for businesses in India. By leveraging data-driven insights, personalized content, and strategic partnerships, Zomato, Nykaa, and Paytm have successfully driven growth and established themselves as leaders in their respective industries.

Benefits of Performance Marketing

1. Cost-effectiveness: Performance marketing is a cost-effective option for businesses as advertisers only pay for the desired results. This pricing model reduces the risk of wasted ad spend and ensures that marketing budgets are used efficiently.

2. Measurable outcomes: Performance marketing provides clear, quantifiable metrics, enabling businesses to track the success of their campaigns and measure ROI accurately. This data-driven approach allows marketers to make informed decisions and allocate resources more effectively.

3. Flexibility and scalability: Performance marketing campaigns can be easily adjusted and scaled based on real-time results. This adaptability allows businesses to respond to market trends and change customer behaviors quickly.

4. Increased brand exposure: By partnering with publishers and influencers, performance marketing can increase brand visibility and reach potential customers who might not be accessible through traditional marketing channels.

5. Improved customer targeting: The advanced targeting capabilities of performance marketing enable businesses to reach specific audience segments more effectively, resulting in higher-quality leads and increased conversions.

Challenges and Best Practices

1. Fraud prevention: Performance marketing can be susceptible to fraudulent activities, such as click fraud or fake leads. To mitigate these risks, businesses should use reliable tracking and reporting tools, implement strict publisher vetting processes, and monitor campaigns closely for any suspicious activities.

2. Maintaining brand integrity: When partnering with publishers or influencers, businesses should ensure that their brand values align with those of the publisher to maintain brand integrity and avoid any negative associations.

3. Balancing short-term and long-term goals: Performance marketing is often focused on immediate results, but businesses should also consider long-term strategies, such as brand building and customer loyalty. Integrating performance marketing with other marketing efforts can help strike this balance and ensure sustainable growth.

4. A/B testing and experimentation: To optimize performance marketing campaigns, businesses should continuously test different ad creatives, targeting options, and bidding strategies. A/B testing and experimentation can help identify the most effective tactics and drive better results over time.

5. Building strong relationships with publishers: Cultivating strong relationships with publishers and influencers is crucial to the success of performance marketing campaigns. By working closely with partners, businesses can ensure better ad placements, negotiate favorable terms and gain access to valuable insights and feedback.

6. Prioritizing user experience: While performance marketing can drive immediate results, it's essential not to compromise user experience in the pursuit of conversions. Intrusive or irrelevant ads can damage brand reputation and turn potential customers away. Businesses should prioritize delivering value and relevant content to users.

7. Investing in technology and tools: Performance marketing relies on accurate tracking and reporting to measure success and optimize campaigns. Businesses should invest in the right technology and tools, such as analytics platforms, CRM systems, and marketing automation software, to effectively manage and analyze campaign data.

Performance marketing has become an essential component of modern digital marketing strategies. By focusing on measurable results and data-driven optimization, businesses can maximize their ROI, reach new customers, and scale their marketing efforts effectively. By understanding the fundamentals of performance marketing, leveraging various channels, and implementing best practices, businesses can harness the power of this innovative marketing approach to drive sustainable growth.

Performance marketing has emerged as a powerful strategy for businesses looking to drive growth and maximize ROI in the digital age. By leveraging the right channels, strategies, and tools, marketers can create highly targeted and data-driven campaigns that deliver measurable results.

As the digital landscape continues to evolve, performance marketing will continue to play a crucial role in helping businesses adapt and thrive. By staying ahead of industry trends and embracing innovation, marketers can ensure their campaigns remain effective and drive long-term success for their brands.

Adapting Global Marketing Strategies to the Indian Context

India is a diverse and rapidly growing market with unique cultural, linguistic, and socioeconomic characteristics. For businesses looking to expand their global marketing efforts, it is crucial to adapt their strategies to resonate with the Indian audience. The following steps outline how to tailor global marketing strategies to the Indian context effectively:

> Understand the market: India is a complex market, with more than 1.3 billion people, over 2,000 distinct ethnic

groups, and 22 officially recognized languages. To succeed in this market, businesses must invest time and resources in understanding the nuances of India's demographics, culture, and consumer behavior. This includes researching regional differences, preferences, and trends that may impact marketing efforts.

One such example of a company that successfully understood the Indian market is Unilever. Unilever, the global consumer goods giant, has been operating in India for decades through its subsidiary, Hindustan Unilever Limited (HUL). The company has been successful in the Indian market because it has invested time and resources into understanding the unique needs and preferences of Indian consumers across different segments and regions.

For instance, HUL conducted extensive market research and realized that affordability was a major concern for many consumers in rural India. To cater to this segment, the company introduced small, affordable sachets of its popular products like shampoo, detergent, and toothpaste. These low-priced sachets made HUL products accessible to a wider consumer base and significantly boosted sales in rural areas.

Additionally, HUL understood that the Indian market is diverse, with significant variations in language, culture, and preferences across different regions. As a result, the company tailored its advertising and marketing campaigns to resonate with different target audiences, often using regional languages and cultural nuances to create a strong connection with consumers.

Unilever's success in the Indian market can be largely attributed to its efforts to understand the market and adapt its products, packaging, pricing, and marketing strategies accordingly.

> Customize the product or service offering: Global businesses must evaluate if their existing products or services align with the needs and preferences of Indian consumers. In some cases, it may be necessary to modify the offering to cater to local tastes, preferences, or cultural sensitivities. For example, McDonald's adapted its menu in India by offering a range of vegetarian options and removing beef and pork products to cater to the predominantly vegetarian population.

Customizing the product or service offering is crucial when entering the Indian market, as it allows companies to cater to the unique needs and preferences of local consumers. A great example of this approach is McDonald's India. When McDonald's entered the Indian market, they understood that they needed to adapt their product offerings to cater to local tastes and preferences.

India has a large vegetarian population, and the consumption of beef is culturally and religiously restricted in many parts of the country. Therefore, McDonald's introduced a range of vegetarian options and replaced beef with chicken in many of their popular items, such as the Maharaja Mac, which is the Indian version of the Big Mac.

McDonald's also incorporated local flavors and ingredients into their menu, with items like the McPaneer Royale, McAloo Tikki, and McSpicy Paneer, specifically designed for the Indian palate. This strategy of customizing their product offerings to cater to local tastes has been crucial in helping McDonald's establish a strong presence in the Indian market and appeal to a broad range of consumers.

> Develop a localized communication strategy: To connect with the Indian audience, businesses need to create marketing messages that resonate with their values, culture, and aspirations. This may involve using regional languages, incorporating local idioms, and referencing cultural touchpoints. For instance, Coca-Cola's advertising campaigns in India often feature popular Indian celebrities and emphasize themes such as togetherness, happiness, and celebrations to appeal to the local audience.

KFC (Kentucky Fried Chicken) is another example of a global brand that has successfully developed a localized communication strategy for the Indian market. When KFC entered India, they understood the importance of adapting their marketing and communication strategies to cater to the diverse and unique preferences of Indian consumers.

One of the most significant changes KFC made was to introduce a variety of vegetarian options in addition to their traditional chicken offerings. They understood that a large portion of the Indian population is vegetarian and created menu items such as the Veg Zinger, Paneer Zinger, and Veg Rice Bowl to cater to this segment.

Moreover, KFC adapted its advertising and promotional campaigns to resonate with the local audience. They used popular Indian celebrities, such as Bollywood actors and cricket players, in their advertisements to build a strong connection with consumers. They also localized their taglines and messaging, using colloquial language and cultural references that were relatable to the Indian audience.

By developing a localized communication strategy, KFC has managed to establish a strong presence in the Indian market and appeal to a wide range of consumers across the country.

> Leverage local insights for content creation: Creating content that is relevant and relatable to the Indian audience is crucial for successful marketing campaigns. Businesses should work with local experts, influencers, or creative agencies to develop content that captures the essence of the Indian market. This may include using local storytelling techniques, incorporating regional humor, or showcasing real-life scenarios that the target audience can relate to.

In 2017, Spotify launched its service in India. Being a country with diverse languages, cultures, and music preferences, Spotify had to adapt its content strategy to cater to the Indian market. To do so, Spotify partnered with local musicians, music labels, and content creators to curate playlists that catered to the tastes of Indian listeners. They also launched a "Desi Hub," which featured Indian music, including regional languages such as Hindi, Tamil, Punjabi, and more. Spotify also created content that was relevant to Indian listeners.

For example, they launched a podcast called "22 Yarns with Gaurav Kapur" which featured conversations with Indian cricketers. This content resonated with Indian users and helped Spotify to establish itself in the market. Overall, Spotify's localized content strategy allowed them to understand and cater to the unique preferences of Indian users, leading to their successful launch in the Indian market.

> Optimize for mobile-first experiences: India has one of the highest smartphone penetration rates globally, with a majority of users accessing the internet through mobile devices. Therefore, businesses must prioritize mobile-first experiences when designing websites, apps, or digital marketing campaigns. This includes optimizing content for mobile viewing, ensuring fast load times, and leveraging mobile-specific ad formats and targeting options.

Paytm, India's leading digital wallet and e-commerce company, optimized its platform for mobile users by creating a mobile app that provides a seamless experience for users. They recognized that mobile usage was rapidly growing in India and focused on creating a platform that is optimized for mobile-first experiences.

Paytm's app is designed to be easy to use and navigate, with a simple and intuitive user interface that is optimized for smaller screens. They also offer a range of features that are specifically designed for mobile users, such as QR code scanning and one-click payments.

This focus on mobile-first experiences has been a key factor in Paytm's success in India, as it has enabled them to capture a large share of the rapidly growing mobile payments market. By making it easy for users to make payments and conduct transactions using their mobile devices, Paytm has become one of the most popular digital wallet providers in India, with over 350 million registered users.

Leverage digital channels and social media platforms: India has a thriving digital ecosystem, with over 500 million internet users and a rapidly growing social media user base. To tap into this massive audience, businesses must focus on digital channels such as search, display, and video advertising, as well as social media platforms like Facebook, Instagram, Twitter, and LinkedIn. Additionally, they should consider the rising popularity of regional social media platforms and messaging apps such as ShareChat and WhatsApp to engage with the local audience.

In 2016, PepsiCo launched a campaign for their brand Kurkure, a popular snack in India, called "Tedha Hai Par Mera Hai" (Roughly translates to "It may be crooked, but it's mine"). The campaign focused on celebrating quirks and individuality, encouraging consumers to embrace their unique personalities. To reach a wider audience, Kurkure leveraged social media platforms such as Facebook, Twitter, and Instagram to create a buzz around the campaign. They also created short videos featuring popular social media influencers who shared their own quirks and encouraged their followers to do the same. Additionally, Kurkure launched a mobile app called "Kurkure Twist Mobile Game," where users could play games and win prizes. The app was promoted through digital channels such as display ads, search ads, and social media ads, reaching millions of users across India. By leveraging digital channels and social media platforms, Kurkure was able to create a successful campaign that resonated with its target audience, resulting in increased brand awareness and sales.

Establish strong partnerships and distribution networks: Building strong partnerships with local businesses, distributors, or retail partners can help global brands establish a foothold in the Indian market. These partners can provide valuable insights, connections, and support to navigate the complexities of the Indian business landscape. Additionally, companies should explore opportunities to collaborate with local influencers, celebrities, or content creators to amplify their marketing efforts and gain credibility among the target audience.

In 2016, Coca-Cola India launched a new variant of its popular Maaza mango drink called Maaza Gold, which was positioned as a premium offering. To reach its target audience of young adults and urban consumers, Coca-Cola India partnered with popular food delivery platform Swiggy to offer Maaza Gold as an exclusive add-on to customers who ordered meals from select restaurants in major cities like Mumbai, Delhi, and Bangalore. This strategic partnership allowed Coca-Cola India to leverage Swiggy's wide user base and delivery network to distribute Maaza Gold to its target audience in a convenient and accessible manner. The campaign was a success, with Maaza Gold quickly becoming one of the top-selling beverages on Swiggy's platform. By partnering with a popular and relevant distribution network, Coca-Cola India was able to expand its reach and sales of its premium product effectively.

Emphasize value and affordability: Price sensitivity is a significant factor in the Indian market, and consumers often prioritize value and affordability when making purchase decisions. Businesses should consider offering competitive pricing, discounts, or promotional offers to attract price-conscious consumers. Additionally, they should focus on highlighting the value proposition of their products or services to demonstrate how they address the needs and pain points of the Indian audience.

One example of a company that emphasizes value and affordability in the Indian market is Patanjali Ayurved Limited. Patanjali is a consumer goods company that specializes in natural and ayurvedic products. The company was founded in 2006 by Baba Ramdev, a renowned yoga guru, and Acharya Balkrishna. Patanjali's products are made from natural and herbal ingredients, which the company claims are of superior quality and more affordable than other similar products in the market. The company leverages its direct-to-consumer sales model, which eliminates the need for intermediaries and reduces costs. Patanjali has also established partnerships with various retailers, including supermarkets and online marketplaces, to expand its distribution network. The company has a strong social media presence and has leveraged digital channels to reach and engage with its customers. Patanjali's emphasis on value and affordability has helped it gain a loyal customer base and establish itself as a leading player in the Indian consumer goods market.

> Monitor performance and adapt: Given the dynamic nature of the Indian market, it is essential to continuously monitor marketing performance and adapt strategies based on data-driven insights. Businesses should regularly track key performance indicators (KPIs) such as reach, engagement,

conversions, and return on investment (ROI) to gauge the effectiveness of their marketing efforts. By analyzing this data, they can identify trends, opportunities, and areas for improvement.

Be culturally sensitive and socially responsible: Indian consumers are increasingly aware of social and environmental issues and expect businesses to be responsible corporate citizens. Companies should ensure that their marketing efforts are culturally sensitive and avoid any content that could be considered offensive or disrespectful. Moreover, they should focus on showcasing their commitment to social responsibility and sustainability, as this can help build trust and credibility among the Indian audience.

In conclusion, adapting global marketing strategies to the Indian context requires a deep understanding of the local market, culture, and consumer behavior. By tailoring their product offerings, communication strategies, and marketing channels to cater to the unique needs and preferences of the Indian audience, businesses can effectively tap into the immense growth potential of this burgeoning market. By being agile, data-driven, and culturally sensitive, global brands can successfully navigate the complexities of the Indian market and establish a strong presence in one of the world's fastest-growing economies.

7

Luxury Brand Management in India

Challenges and Opportunities in India's Luxury Market

India's luxury market has witnessed significant growth over the past few years, driven by its expanding affluent population, increasing disposable incomes, and rapid urbanization. Despite this promising outlook, luxury brands face several challenges in India. However, with the right strategies and understanding of the market, brands can capitalize on the vast opportunities that the Indian luxury market has to offer.

Challenges

a. High import duties and taxes: Import duties and taxes on luxury goods in India are among the highest in the world. This results in exorbitant retail prices, discouraging potential buyers and limiting the growth of the luxury market.

b. Limited availability of prime retail spaces: India's urban infrastructure, especially in major cities like Mumbai, Delhi, and Bangalore, is underdeveloped, leading to a shortage of prime retail spaces suitable for luxury stores. This poses a significant challenge for luxury brands looking to establish a physical presence in the country.

c. Counterfeiting and grey market: The Indian luxury market faces a significant challenge from counterfeit products and grey market imports. This not only tarnishes the image of luxury brands but also results in substantial revenue losses.

d. Cultural and regional differences: India is a diverse country with a myriad of languages, customs, and preferences. Navigating this cultural diversity can be challenging for luxury brands, especially when trying to create a consistent brand image and positioning.

e. Limited awareness of luxury brands: Many Indian consumers are still unfamiliar with international luxury brands, especially those that have not been widely publicized or marketed in the country. This lack of awareness can hinder the growth of luxury brands in the market.

Opportunities

a. Growing affluent population: India's middle and upper classes are growing rapidly, with an increasing number of people possessing the financial means to afford luxury goods and experiences. This presents an enormous opportunity for luxury brands to tap into this expanding consumer base.

b. Digitalization and e-commerce: The rapid growth of the internet and digital platforms in India offers luxury brands a unique opportunity to engage with their target audience and expand their reach. E-commerce platforms, in particular, provide an avenue for luxury brands to increase their sales and visibility.

c. Focus on experiences: Indian consumers are increasingly valuing experiences over material possessions. Luxury brands can capitalize on this trend by offering unique, personalized, and immersive experiences that go beyond their products, such as exclusive events, workshops, or travel experiences.

d. Customization and personalization: Indian consumers appreciate a sense of exclusivity and uniqueness in their luxury purchases. Luxury brands can cater to this preference by offering personalized and customized products or services, which can help them differentiate themselves from competitors and strengthen their brand image.

e. Collaborations and partnerships: Luxury brands can forge strategic collaborations and partnerships with local designers, artists, or other businesses to create unique, India-inspired products or experiences. These collaborations can not only help luxury brands gain a better understanding of the Indian market but also enhance their brand image and appeal to local consumers.

In conclusion, while the Indian luxury market presents several challenges, it also offers immense opportunities for growth and expansion. Luxury brands that can effectively navigate these challenges and capitalize on the market's unique opportunities will be well-positioned to succeed and thrive in this dynamic and rapidly evolving market.

Strategies for Establishing and Managing Luxury Brands in India

As the Indian luxury market continues to grow, it presents tremendous opportunities for luxury brands to establish and expand their presence. However, navigating the Indian market can be challenging due to its unique cultural, economic, and regulatory landscape. This chapter outlines key strategies for successfully establishing and managing luxury brands in India.

1. Understanding the Indian consumer: Before entering the Indian market, it is crucial for luxury brands to gain a deep understanding of the Indian consumer's preferences, attitudes, and behaviors. This includes being aware of regional differences, cultural nuances, and varying tastes. Conducting thorough market research, including surveys and focus groups, can help brands gain valuable insights into the Indian consumer psyche and tailor their products and marketing strategies accordingly.

2. Localizing the brand offering: To appeal to the Indian consumer, luxury brands should consider localizing their product offerings by incorporating elements that reflect Indian tastes, culture, and heritage. This can include using Indian textiles, motifs, or colors in products or partnering with local designers and artisans to create exclusive, India-inspired collections. Localizing the brand offering not only makes it more appealing to the Indian consumer but also helps differentiate the brand in a competitive market.

3. Establishing a strong brand identity: Creating a strong and consistent brand identity is crucial for luxury brands to establish themselves in the Indian market. This includes focusing on the brand's unique selling proposition (USP), such as superior craftsmanship, exclusivity, or heritage, and communicating it effectively through advertising, public relations, and in-store experiences. Additionally, luxury brands should consider collaborating with Indian celebrities or influencers to enhance their brand visibility and credibility.

4. Selecting the right retail channels: Selecting the right retail channels is critical for luxury brands to reach their target audience and establish a strong presence in the Indian market. This can include setting up flagship stores in prime locations, partnering with luxury malls or department stores, or leveraging e-commerce platforms. Brands should carefully consider their target audience, product offerings, and brand positioning when selecting the most suitable retail channels.

5. Investing in digital marketing and e-commerce: With the rapid growth of internet users and digital platforms in India, investing in digital marketing and e-commerce is essential for luxury brands to engage with their target audience and expand their reach. Brands should create an engaging online presence through well-designed websites, social media platforms, and targeted digital advertising campaigns. Additionally, luxury brands should consider partnering with established e-commerce platforms or developing their e-commerce capabilities to tap into the growing online market.

6. Focusing on customer experience: Indian consumers are increasingly valuing experiences over material possessions, making it essential for luxury brands to focus on delivering exceptional customer experiences. This can include offering personalized services, organizing exclusive events, or providing immersive in-store experiences that reflect the brand's values and heritage. By focusing on customer experience, luxury brands can create lasting impressions and build customer loyalty.

7. Adapting to regulatory challenges: Navigating India's complex regulatory environment, including high import duties and taxes, can be challenging for luxury brands. Brands should stay informed about the latest regulations and adapt their strategies accordingly, such as sourcing materials locally or setting up manufacturing units in India to reduce import costs.

8. Developing a strong after-sales service network: Providing excellent after-sales service is crucial for building customer trust and loyalty in the luxury segment. Luxury brands should invest in developing a strong after-sales service network, including dedicated service centers, trained personnel, and seamless customer support. This not only helps enhance customer satisfaction but also positions the brand as a reliable and trustworthy player in the market.

9. Monitoring and adapting to market trends: The Indian luxury market is constantly evolving, and luxury brands must stay abreast of the latest trends and developments to remain competitive. This includes monitoring consumer preferences, emerging competitors, and industry innovations. By staying informed and

adapting their strategies accordingly, luxury brands can stay ahead of the curve and maintain their relevance in the market.

10. Building long-term relationships with customers: Cultivating long-term relationships with customers is crucial for luxury brands to ensure repeat business and customer loyalty. This can be achieved through personalized communication, exclusive offers, and loyalty programs tailored to the needs and preferences of the Indian consumer. By fostering long-term relationships, luxury brands can create a loyal customer base and ensure sustainable growth in the Indian market.

11. Collaborating with local talent and resources: Establishing partnerships with local talent and resources can help luxury brands gain valuable insights into the Indian market and improve their offerings. This can include collaborating with local designers, artisans, or even educational institutions to develop new products, conduct market research, or train the workforce. By leveraging local talent and resources, luxury brands can adapt more effectively to the Indian market and ensure their products and services resonate with the local consumer.

12. Engaging in corporate social responsibility (CSR) initiatives: Indian consumers are increasingly conscious of the social and environmental impact of their consumption choices, making it essential for luxury brands to engage in CSR initiatives. By aligning their CSR efforts with local causes and concerns, luxury brands can not only enhance their brand image but also create a positive impact on the communities they operate in. Examples

of CSR initiatives can include promoting sustainable practices, supporting local artisans, or engaging in philanthropic activities.

In conclusion, establishing and managing luxury brands in India requires a deep understanding of the local market, adaptation of strategies to cater to the unique preferences and challenges of the Indian consumer, and a focus on delivering exceptional customer experiences. By following the strategies outlined in this chapter, luxury brands can successfully navigate the Indian market and achieve sustainable growth.

Case studies of successful luxury brands in India

In this section, we will examine some successful case studies of luxury brands that have effectively entered and established themselves in the Indian market. These examples demonstrate how these luxury brands have adapted their strategies to cater to the unique preferences, tastes, and challenges of the Indian consumer.

1. Louis Vuitton

Louis Vuitton is a well-known luxury fashion brand that has made significant inroads into the Indian market. The brand's success can be attributed to its focus on innovation and adaptation to local market trends while maintaining its global brand identity.

One of Louis Vuitton's most successful marketing strategies in India has been its digital marketing campaigns. The brand has been leveraging social media platforms like Instagram and Facebook to reach out to a wider audience and build brand awareness. It has also been using influencer marketing to tap into local audiences and build a loyal customer base.

Another strategy that Louis Vuitton has used to succeed in the Indian market is its focus on personalization. The brand has been offering customized products and services that cater to the unique needs and preferences of Indian consumers. For example, Louis Vuitton has launched a 'Make it Yours' campaign that allows customers to personalize their handbags by selecting their preferred colors, materials, and design elements.

Louis Vuitton has also been expanding its physical presence in India by opening flagship stores in key cities like Mumbai and New Delhi. These stores offer an immersive brand experience that allows customers to engage with the brand on a more personal level.

Overall, Louis Vuitton's success in the Indian market can be attributed to its ability to adapt to local market trends while maintaining its global brand identity, its focus on digital marketing and personalization, and its investment in physical retail spaces to create a unique brand experience for its customers.

2. Burberry

Burberry is a British luxury fashion brand that has established a strong presence in the Indian market. The brand's success in India can be attributed to its focus on digital innovation, customer engagement, and personalized experiences.

One of Burberry's key strategies in India is its emphasis on digital innovation. The brand has leveraged technology to create a seamless omnichannel experience for customers, allowing them to transition seamlessly between online and offline shopping. Burberry has also invested in creating engaging digital experiences for customers, such as its AR-powered "Burberry World Live" platform, which allows users to explore the brand's collections and events in a 3D virtual space.

Burberry has also focused on customer engagement and personalization in its Indian marketing efforts. The brand has tailored its marketing campaigns to the Indian market, creating ads and social media content that resonate with local audiences. Burberry has also launched a number of initiatives to engage with customers, such as its "Art of the Trench" project, which invites customers to share photos of themselves wearing Burberry trench coats.

In addition to its marketing efforts, Burberry has also invested in creating personalized experiences for customers in its Indian stores. The brand's stores feature interactive displays, personalized styling services, and exclusive collections, all designed to create a luxurious and immersive shopping experience.

Burberry's focus on digital innovation, customer engagement, and personalized experiences has helped the brand establish a strong presence in the Indian luxury market. By staying attuned to the needs and preferences of Indian consumers and leveraging technology to create seamless experiences, Burberry has positioned itself as a leader in the Indian luxury fashion industry.

3. BMW

BMW is a luxury car brand that has been operating in India since 2006. Over the years, the brand has established a strong presence in the Indian luxury car market thanks to its innovative marketing and branding strategies.

One of the key strategies that BMW has leveraged to attract Indian customers is localization. The company has localized its products to cater to the unique needs and preferences of the Indian market. For example, the BMW 3 Series Gran Turismo was launched in India in 2014 with a higher ground clearance to suit Indian road conditions. Similarly, the BMW X1, a luxury SUV, was also launched in India with a diesel engine to cater to the Indian market's preference for diesel-powered vehicles.

In addition to product localization, BMW has also leveraged digital marketing and social media to reach out to its target audience. The company has a strong presence on social media platforms such as Facebook, Twitter, and Instagram, where it shares updates on its latest products and promotions. To engage with its customers on a deeper level, BMW has also launched a loyalty program called BMW Excellence Club. The program offers exclusive benefits to BMW customers, including access to exclusive events and experiences.

Furthermore, BMW has also leveraged data-driven decision-making to optimize its marketing and sales efforts. The company uses customer data and analytics to understand consumer preferences and behavior, which helps it to develop targeted marketing campaigns and sales strategies.

In conclusion, BMW's success in the Indian luxury car market can be attributed to its focus on localization, digital marketing, customer engagement, and data-driven decision-making. By understanding the unique needs and preferences of the Indian market and leveraging the latest technologies, BMW has established itself as one of the leading luxury car brands in India.

4. Taj Hotels

Taj Hotels is a luxury hotel chain based in India. The company was founded in 1903 and has since grown to become one of the most well-known and respected hotel brands in the world. Taj Hotels is part of the Tata Group, a multinational conglomerate with diverse business interests.

Taj Hotels has always been known for its commitment to exceptional service and attention to detail. However, the company recognized that it needed to evolve its marketing strategy to remain competitive in an increasingly crowded market. Taj Hotels decided to focus on digital marketing and social media to reach a wider audience and engage with customers in new ways.

One of the key initiatives that Taj Hotels implemented was a comprehensive social media strategy. The company created a presence on multiple social media platforms, including Facebook, Twitter, and Instagram, and began actively engaging with followers. Taj Hotels used social media to showcase its properties, highlight events and promotions, and share content that would be of interest to its target audience.

In addition to social media, Taj Hotels also invested in digital advertising. The company used targeted advertising campaigns to reach potential customers and drive bookings. Taj Hotels analyzed customer data to identify key demographics and create personalized campaigns that would resonate with specific audiences.

Taj Hotels also utilized technology to improve the guest experience. The company introduced a mobile app that allowed guests to book rooms, make reservations at restaurants and spas, and access hotel information and services. The app also provided real-time updates on events and promotions, allowing guests to stay informed and engaged during their stay.

These initiatives paid off for Taj Hotels. The company saw a significant increase in online bookings, as well as an increase in brand awareness and engagement on social media. Taj Hotels also received positive feedback from guests who appreciated the convenience and personalized experience provided by the mobile app.

Overall, Taj Hotels' use of technology and data-driven decision-making has helped the company remain competitive in a challenging market. By leveraging social media, digital advertising, and mobile technology, Taj Hotels has been able to reach new audiences and engage with customers in new and innovative ways.

5. Titan's Tanishq

Tanishq, a jewelry brand owned by Titan Company Limited, is one of India's most successful luxury brands. Tanishq has established itself as a premium jewelry brand with a wide range of collections, including gold, diamond, and platinum jewelry. The brand's success can be attributed to its ability to cater to the evolving tastes of Indian consumers and offer high-quality products at affordable prices.

One of Tanishq's most successful campaigns was the "Remarriage" campaign, launched in 2013. The campaign aimed to break the social stigma surrounding remarriage in India and promote the idea of second marriages. Tanishq partnered with Ogilvy & Mather to create a powerful ad that featured a beautiful bride getting ready for her remarriage.

The ad received widespread acclaim and was seen as a bold move by a luxury brand. Tanishq has also leveraged social media to connect with its audience and showcase its products. The brand has a strong presence on Instagram, where it shares images of its latest collections and engages with followers. Tanishq has also launched a virtual try-on feature on its website, allowing customers to try on jewelry virtually before making a purchase.

In addition to its product offerings, Tanishq has also invested in customer service and experience. The brand has established over 300 retail stores across India, providing a seamless and personalized shopping experience to customers. Tanishq's stores are known for their elegant interiors and knowledgeable staff, who assist customers in choosing the perfect piece of jewelry.

Overall, Tanishq's success can be attributed to its ability to stay relevant and innovative in a highly competitive market. The brand's commitment to quality, affordability, and customer experience has helped it establish itself as one of India's leading luxury brands.

8

Embracing Cultural and Demographic Diversity

India's Cultural and Demographic Landscape

India, with its rich cultural and demographic diversity, presents both opportunities and challenges for businesses looking to establish and grow in the country. The nation is home to more than 1.3 billion people, making it the second most populous country in the world. This vast population is characterized by a multitude of languages, religions, and ethnic groups, each with its unique traditions, customs, and preferences. To succeed in the Indian market, businesses must understand and embrace this cultural and demographic landscape and tailor their strategies accordingly.

Languages: India is a linguistically diverse country, with more than 19,500 languages and dialects spoken across its 28 states and 8 union territories. The Indian constitution recognizes 22 official languages, including Hindi, English, Bengali, Telugu, Marathi, Tamil, Urdu, and Gujarati, among others. While Hindi is the most widely spoken language, English serves as a lingua franca, particularly in urban areas and among the educated population. For businesses operating in India, it is crucial to adopt a multilingual approach to cater to the language preferences of their target audience. This includes developing marketing materials, product packaging, and customer support services in multiple languages, as well as employing a diverse workforce with language skills that reflect the diversity of the Indian market.

Religions: India is a secular country that is home to a variety of religious beliefs and practices. The major religions in India are Hinduism, Islam, Christianity, and Sikhism, which collectively account for over 99% of the population. In addition, there are smaller religious groups, such as Buddhists, Jains, Parsis, and Jews, each with its unique customs and traditions. Understanding the religious landscape of India is essential for businesses, as it influences consumer behavior, preferences, and purchasing decisions. Businesses must be sensitive to religious sentiments and develop products and marketing strategies that respect and accommodate the beliefs and values of their target audience. This may include offering products that cater to specific religious dietary restrictions or incorporating religious symbols and messages in marketing campaigns during festive seasons.

Ethnic Groups: India is home to numerous ethnic groups, each with its distinct culture, traditions, and customs. These ethnic groups are often defined by their geographic location, language, and historical background. Some of the major ethnic groups in India include the Indo-Aryans, Dravidians, Tibeto-Burmans, and Austroasiatic groups.

Each ethnic group has its unique preferences and tastes, which can influence consumer behavior and purchasing decisions. Businesses must be aware of these differences and develop products and marketing strategies that cater to the unique needs and preferences of each ethnic group. This may include offering region-specific products, utilizing local influencers and endorsers, and adopting marketing messages that resonate with the target audience's cultural background.

Demographics: India's demographics are characterized by a young and growing population, with more than 65% of the population under the age of 35. This demographic shift has significant implications for businesses, as it presents opportunities to target a large and growing consumer base with disposable income and a willingness to spend on new products and experiences. To capitalize on this demographic trend, businesses must develop products and marketing strategies that cater to the preferences and lifestyles of young Indian consumers. This may include focusing on digital platforms and social media for marketing, offering innovative and aspirational products, and incorporating elements of Indian pop culture in branding and advertising.

In conclusion, understanding and embracing India's cultural and demographic landscape is essential for businesses looking to succeed in the Indian market. By developing products and marketing strategies that cater to the unique preferences and needs of the diverse Indian population, businesses can tap into the immense growth potential that the country offers.

Adapting Products and Services to Cater to Diverse Segments

In today's globalized world, catering to the diverse needs and preferences of different customer segments is essential for businesses looking to succeed in competitive markets. The Indian market, in particular, with its vast cultural and demographic diversity, demands a tailored approach to product and service offerings. Adapting products and services to cater to diverse segments requires a deep understanding of the target audience and a willingness to innovate and evolve. In this section, we will discuss various strategies for adapting products and services to cater to diverse segments in the Indian market.

Conduct thorough market research: Understanding the preferences, needs, and aspirations of the target audience is critical for adapting products and services to cater to diverse segments. Market research can help businesses gather valuable insights into customer demographics, preferences, and purchasing behaviors. This information can then be used to design and develop products and services that resonate with the target audience. Market research can be conducted through various channels, including surveys, interviews, focus groups, and online data analysis.

Customize product offerings: Customizing product offerings to cater to the unique needs and preferences of different customer segments is essential for businesses operating in diverse markets. This may involve modifying existing products or developing new products that appeal to specific customer segments. For example, food and beverage companies may offer products with different flavors or spice levels to cater to regional tastes. Similarly, fashion and apparel brands may develop collections that incorporate regional styles and designs, while technology companies may offer devices with region-specific features and applications.

Tailor marketing and branding strategies: Adapting marketing and branding strategies to cater to diverse customer segments is crucial for businesses looking to succeed in the Indian market. This may involve developing marketing messages that resonate with the target audience's cultural background and values, using local influencers and endorsers, and leveraging regional media and advertising platforms. In addition, businesses should consider using local languages and cultural references in their marketing materials, as well as incorporating region-specific themes and designs in their branding and packaging.

Develop inclusive pricing strategies: Pricing strategies play a significant role in catering to diverse customer segments, as different segments may have varying purchasing power and price sensitivities. Businesses should consider offering products and services at different price points to cater to a broad range of customers. This may include offering budget-friendly options for price-conscious consumers, as well as premium products for customers seeking luxury and exclusivity. Developing flexible and inclusive pricing strategies can help businesses attract a diverse customer base and maximize their market potential.

Offer personalized services: Offering personalized services is an effective way to cater to diverse customer segments and build lasting relationships with customers. Businesses can provide personalized services by understanding the individual needs and preferences of their customers and tailoring their offerings accordingly. This may include offering customized product recommendations, providing personalized customer support, and delivering tailored content and promotions. By offering personalized services, businesses can create a unique and memorable customer experience that sets them apart from their competitors.

Leverage technology and data analytics: Technology and data analytics can play a crucial role in helping businesses adapt their products and services to cater to diverse customer segments. By analyzing customer data, businesses can gain valuable insights into customer preferences, needs, and behaviors, which can then be used to inform product development, marketing, and sales strategies. Furthermore, technology can help businesses streamline their operations and improve their ability to cater to diverse customer segments. For example, e-commerce platforms can use algorithms to personalize product recommendations based on customer browsing and purchase history, while customer relationship management (CRM) systems can help businesses manage customer interactions and deliver personalized experiences.

Invest in local partnerships and collaborations: Forming partnerships and collaborations with local businesses, organizations, and influencers can help businesses better understand and cater to diverse customer segments. Local partners can provide valuable insights into regional preferences and trends, as well as help businesses navigate cultural nuances and regulatory requirements. Moreover, collaborating with local partners can enhance a business's credibility and appeal among the target audience, as customers are more likely to trust and support businesses that are seen as invested in their community.

Foster cultural sensitivity and inclusivity within the organization: To effectively cater to diverse customer segments, businesses must foster a culture of sensitivity and inclusivity within their organization. This involves ensuring that employees are trained and educated on cultural differences, biases, and stereotypes and that they are encouraged to approach their work with empathy and understanding. Creating an inclusive and culturally sensitive work environment can help businesses better understand and serve their diverse customer base, as well as foster innovation and creativity within the organization.

In conclusion, adapting products and services to cater to diverse customer segments is essential for businesses operating in the Indian market. By understanding the unique needs and preferences of different customer segments, businesses can tailor their offerings to resonate with their target audience and maximize their market potential. Implementing the strategies discussed in this section can help businesses succeed in the diverse and competitive Indian market.

Creating Inclusive Marketing Campaigns

Inclusive marketing targets all consumers regardless of their race, ethnicity, gender, sexual orientation, age, ability, or other characteristics. It aims to create advertising and marketing campaigns that resonate with a diverse range of consumers and avoid stereotypes or discrimination in marketing messages. Inclusive marketing aims to build brand loyalty and foster positive relationships between companies and diverse consumer segments by demonstrating a commitment to diversity, equity, and inclusion.

In an increasingly diverse and interconnected world, businesses need to ensure that their marketing campaigns are inclusive and resonate with their diverse customer base. Inclusive marketing not only helps businesses tap into new market segments but also enhances their brand image and fosters customer loyalty. This section will discuss strategies for creating inclusive marketing campaigns that cater to diverse audiences in the Indian context.

Understand your audience

The first step in creating an inclusive marketing campaign is to understand your target audience's diverse needs, preferences, and expectations. This involves conducting market research and gathering data on customer demographics, cultural backgrounds, socio-economic status, and other relevant factors. By understanding your audience's unique needs and preferences, you can create marketing campaigns that resonate with them and reflect their values.

Develop culturally sensitive content

When developing marketing content, it is essential to be mindful of cultural sensitivities and avoid perpetuating stereotypes, biases, or offensive imagery. Businesses should invest in cultural training for their marketing teams to ensure they are equipped to create culturally sensitive content that appeals to diverse audiences. Additionally, businesses should consult with local experts, community leaders, or cultural consultants to gain insights into cultural nuances and ensure that their marketing content is appropriate and respectful.

Use diverse imagery and representation

One of the most visible aspects of inclusive marketing is the use of diverse imagery and representation in marketing materials. This means featuring people from different backgrounds, ethnicities, genders, ages, and abilities in your marketing campaigns. By showcasing diverse representation in your marketing materials, you send a message that your brand values diversity and inclusivity and that your products and services cater to a broad audience.

Leverage local insights and storytelling

Creating inclusive marketing campaigns also involves leveraging local insights and storytelling to connect with your audience on a deeper level. This means using stories, cultural references, or experiences that are relevant and relatable to your diverse audience. By incorporating local insights and storytelling into your marketing campaigns, you can create a sense of connection and authenticity that resonates with your audience.

Adapt messaging and tone for different segments

Adapting your marketing messaging and tone to cater to the unique needs and preferences of different customer segments is essential. This may involve creating tailored marketing materials for different regions, languages, or cultural groups or using different communication styles and channels to reach diverse audiences. Customizing your messaging and tone ensures that your marketing campaigns resonate with your target audience and effectively communicate your brand's value proposition.

Be authentic and transparent

Authenticity and transparency are critical components of inclusive marketing. Businesses should be open and honest about their commitment to diversity and inclusion and should communicate their efforts to promote inclusivity within their organization and marketing campaigns. By being authentic and transparent, businesses can build trust with their diverse customer base and create a positive brand image.

Monitor and measure the impact of your inclusive marketing campaigns

To ensure the effectiveness of your inclusive marketing campaigns, monitoring and measuring their impact is essential. This involves tracking key performance indicators (KPIs) such as engagement, reach, conversions, and customer sentiment. By analyzing the data, businesses can gain insights into their marketing campaigns' effectiveness and identify improvement areas. Moreover, monitoring and measuring the impact of inclusive marketing campaigns can help businesses demonstrate their commitment to diversity and inclusion and showcase their efforts to create more inclusive marketing strategies.

Examples of Inclusive Marketing Campaigns

Brooke Bond Red Label Tea, a brand under Hindustan Unilever Limited (HUL), launched the "6 Pack Band 2.0" campaign in 2018 to promote inclusivity and celebrate diversity in India. The campaign was a sequel to the successful "6 Pack Band" campaign launched in 2016, which featured a band of six transgender singers.

In "6 Pack Band 2.0," Brooke Bond Red Label Tea partnered with Y-Films, the youth wing of Indian film production company Yash Raj Films, to create a band of six specially-abled teenagers who performed popular Bollywood songs with a twist. The band included members with various disabilities, including hearing and speech impairments and Down syndrome.

The campaign aimed to raise awareness about inclusivity and the abilities of differently-abled individuals. The 6 Pack Band 2.0 released six music videos shared on various social media platforms, including YouTube, Facebook, Twitter, and Instagram.

The campaign was a huge success and received widespread praise for its positive message and creative approach. It won several awards, including the Grand Prix for Good at the Cannes Lions International Festival of Creativity in 2018.

Brooke Bond Red Label Tea's "6 Pack Band 2.0" campaign demonstrated the power of inclusive marketing to promote social change and positively impact society. The campaign celebrated the abilities of differently-abled individuals and encouraged viewers to embrace inclusivity and diversity.

Project Free Period by Stayfree was a campaign to address menstrual hygiene and break the stigma around menstruation in India. Stayfree partnered with the NGO, Dasra, to launch the campaign in 2014, which aimed to provide menstrual hygiene education and free sanitary pads to underprivileged girls in India.

Stayfree used various platforms to spread awareness about the campaign, including social media, television, print media, and events.

They launched a hashtag #StayfreeIndia to promote the campaign on social media and encouraged people to share their stories about menstruation. They also organized various events, including street plays and educational workshops in schools, to educate girls about menstrual hygiene.

The campaign garnered immense support and successfully raised awareness about menstrual hygiene and broke the taboo around menstruation in India. Stayfree distributed over 13 million pads to underprivileged girls across India and provided menstrual hygiene education to over 8 lakh girls.

Project Free Period by Stayfree not only positively impacted the lives of underprivileged girls but also helped break the taboo around menstruation and promote inclusive marketing in India.

#ShareTheLoad campaign by Ariel India was launched in 2015 with the aim of promoting gender equality and encouraging men to share the burden of household chores with women. The campaign highlighted the fact that women were expected to do all the household work, including laundry, even while holding down a job, while men were not expected to help.

The campaign included a powerful video that showed a father's realization that he had unintentionally been passing on a biased message to his daughter. The video showed the father asking his daughter for forgiveness and then committing to sharing a load of household chores with his wife.

The campaign was a huge success, with the video being viewed over 50 million times and receiving widespread praise for its powerful message. The campaign sparked conversations on gender roles and traditional biases in India, encouraging other brands to focus on social messaging in their advertising.

Ariel India continued the campaign in 2019 with the #ShareTheLoad Selfie Filter launch, which encouraged people to share pictures of themselves sharing household chores and spreading the message of gender equality. The campaign has since expanded to include partnerships with organizations and NGOs working to promote women's empowerment and gender equality.

The "Touch of Care" campaign by Vicks India is a heartwarming and emotionally impactful campaign that aims to break social stigmas surrounding adoption and family roles in India. The campaign featured a real-life story of a transgender woman named Gauri Sawant, who adopted a young girl named Gayatri.

The video ad showcases Gauri's struggle as a transgender woman to adopt a child and the emotional journey that led her to adopt Gayatri. The ad also highlights the bond between the two as Gayatri calls Gauri her "mother," and Gauri explains how she sees herself as a mother figure to Gayatri.

The campaign was widely successful, with the video ad receiving millions of views and generating significant media coverage. The ad's impact was felt in India and globally, with many praising the message of inclusion and acceptance. The campaign helped to challenge traditional notions of family and parenthood and sparked conversations around the acceptance and inclusion of the transgender community in India.

In conclusion, creating inclusive marketing campaigns is essential for businesses operating in diverse markets such as India. By implementing the strategies discussed in this section, businesses can create marketing campaigns that resonate with their diverse customer base and foster brand loyalty. Inclusive marketing not only helps businesses tap into new market segments but also enhances their brand image and fosters customer loyalty in the long run.

9

Sustainability and Ethical Practices

The Importance of Sustainability and Ethical Practices in Business

Introduction

In today's rapidly changing business environment, sustainability and ethical practices have emerged as key factors that drive long-term success and profitability. Companies that prioritize sustainability and ethical practices contribute positively to society and the environment and enjoy numerous benefits, such as improved brand reputation, customer loyalty, and long-term growth. This sub-chapter will discuss the importance of sustainability and ethical practices in business, focusing on the Indian context.

The Growing Demand for Sustainable and Ethical Products and Services

Consumers, especially the younger generation, are becoming increasingly conscious of the impact of their consumption habits on society and the environment. As a result, there is a growing demand for sustainable and ethical products and services. This shift in consumer preferences presents an opportunity for businesses to differentiate themselves by adopting sustainable and ethical practices, which can lead to increased market share and customer loyalty.

Regulatory and Legal Requirements

Governments worldwide, including India, are introducing stricter regulations and legal requirements to encourage businesses to adopt sustainable and ethical practices. These regulations address various aspects of business operations, such as environmental protection, labor rights, and corporate governance. Compliance with these regulations is not only essential to avoid legal penalties but also to maintain a positive brand image and attract investment.

Enhancing Brand Reputation and Building Trust

Adopting sustainable and ethical practices can significantly enhance a company's brand reputation, helping it stand out in a competitive marketplace. By demonstrating their commitment to sustainability and ethical practices, businesses can build trust with their customers, investors, employees, and other stakeholders, leading to increased loyalty and long-term growth.

Risk Mitigation and Cost Savings

Sustainable and ethical practices can help businesses mitigate various risks, such as reputational damage, supply chain disruptions, and regulatory penalties. By adopting sustainable practices, companies can also achieve cost savings through efficient resource utilization, reduced waste, and lower energy consumption. In addition, ethical practices help businesses avoid potential legal issues, employee attrition, and other costs associated with unethical behavior.

Attracting Investment and Talent

Companies prioritizing sustainability and ethical practices are more likely to attract investment from socially responsible investors, who increasingly consider environmental, social, and governance (ESG) factors when making investment decisions. Additionally, businesses that uphold high ethical standards are more likely to attract and retain top talent, as employees increasingly seek employers that align with their values and contribute positively to society.

Fostering Innovation and Growth

Sustainable and ethical practices can foster innovation and drive growth by encouraging businesses to develop new products, services, and processes that address social and environmental challenges. By embracing sustainability and ethical practices, companies can unlock new market opportunities and create value for their stakeholders while addressing pressing global issues.

Building Resilience and Long-term Value

Companies that prioritize sustainability and ethical practices are more likely to build resilience and create long-term value for their stakeholders. Sustainable and ethical practices can help businesses navigate market volatility, adapt to changing regulations, and respond effectively to environmental and social challenges. By building resilience, businesses can ensure their long-term success and profitability in an increasingly uncertain world.

Conclusion

The importance of sustainability and ethical practices in business cannot be overstated, especially in the context of India's growing economy and diverse market. By prioritizing sustainability and ethical practices, businesses can contribute positively to society and the environment and enjoy numerous benefits, such as improved brand reputation, customer loyalty, and long-term growth. As India continues to develop and evolve, it is essential for businesses to recognize the importance of sustainability and ethical practices and integrate them into their strategies and operations to ensure their long-term success and competitiveness.

Integrating Sustainability into Business Operations and Marketing Strategies

Introduction

Integrating sustainability into business operations and marketing strategies is essential for companies looking to adapt to changing market dynamics and consumer preferences. This sub-chapter provides an in-depth discussion of how businesses can incorporate sustainability into their operations and marketing strategies, leading to long-term success and a positive impact on society and the environment.

Assessing the Current State of Sustainability The first step in integrating sustainability into business operations and marketing strategies is to assess the current state of sustainability within the organization. This involves evaluating the environmental and social impacts of existing processes, products, and services and identifying improvement opportunities. Businesses can use various assessment tools and frameworks, such as the Global Reporting Initiative (GRI) or the Sustainability Accounting Standards Board (SASB), to guide this process.

Establishing Sustainability Goals and Objectives Once the current state of sustainability has been assessed, businesses should establish clear sustainability goals and objectives. These goals should align with the company's overall mission and values and address specific environmental and social issues relevant to the organization's operations. By setting measurable and time-bound targets, businesses can track their progress and ensure that their sustainability efforts remain focused and results-driven.

Developing a Sustainability Strategy With clear sustainability goals and objectives in place, businesses can develop a comprehensive sustainability strategy. This strategy should outline the specific actions and initiatives that the organization will undertake to achieve its sustainability goals. A robust sustainability strategy should address various aspects of business operations, including resource management, waste reduction, energy efficiency, and supply chain management.

Integrating Sustainability into Business Processes To effectively integrate sustainability into business operations, companies must embed sustainable practices into their core processes and decision-making. This may involve re-engineering existing processes, adopting new technologies, or implementing new management systems to ensure that sustainability considerations are integrated throughout the organization. By incorporating sustainability into day-to-day operations, businesses can create a culture of sustainability that permeates the entire organization.

Engaging Employees and Stakeholders Employee engagement is critical for the successful integration of sustainability into business operations and marketing strategies. Companies should invest in training and development programs to educate employees about sustainability issues and the organization's sustainability goals. In addition, businesses should encourage open dialogue and collaboration among employees to generate new ideas and solutions for achieving sustainability objectives.

Stakeholder engagement is also essential, as it helps businesses understand the expectations and concerns of their stakeholders, including customers, investors, suppliers, and communities. By engaging with stakeholders, companies can gather valuable insights and feedback that can inform their sustainability strategies and initiatives.

Integrating Sustainability into Marketing Strategies Integrating sustainability into marketing strategies involves communicating the organization's sustainability efforts and achievements to customers and other stakeholders. Sustainable marketing strategies should focus on promoting the environmental and social benefits of products and services and highlighting the company's commitment to sustainability.

Some effective, sustainable marketing tactics include:

- Developing eco-friendly packaging and promotional materials

- Highlighting the use of sustainable materials and processes in product manufacturing

- Showcasing the company's corporate social responsibility (CSR) initiatives and partnerships

- Utilizing digital marketing channels to reduce the environmental impact of traditional marketing methods

Monitoring and Reporting Progress Regular monitoring and reporting are crucial for ensuring that the organization remains on track to achieve its sustainability goals and objectives. By measuring and reporting progress, businesses can identify areas for improvement and demonstrate their commitment to sustainability to stakeholders.

Conclusion

Integrating sustainability into business operations and marketing strategies is essential for companies looking to adapt to changing market dynamics and consumer preferences. Businesses can effectively incorporate sustainability into their operations by assessing the current state of sustainability, setting clear goals, developing a comprehensive strategy, and embedding sustainable practices into core processes. Furthermore, engaging employees and stakeholders, adopting sustainable marketing tactics, and monitoring and reporting progress are all essential to successful sustainability integration.

When businesses embrace sustainability and ethical practices, they contribute to a better world and enjoy numerous benefits, including enhanced brand reputation, increased customer loyalty, reduced operational costs, and improved risk management. By adopting a proactive approach to sustainability, companies can ensure their long-term success and positively impact society and the environment.

Case studies of sustainable and ethical brands in India

Patagonia: Patagonia is a global leader in the outdoor apparel industry and is widely known for its commitment to sustainability and ethical practices. The brand has gained a strong following among environmentally conscious consumers in India. Patagonia's mission statement, "Build the best product, cause no unnecessary harm, use business to inspire and implement solutions to the environmental crisis," reflects the company's dedication to sustainability. Patagonia actively promotes the repair, reuse, and recycling of its products, encouraging customers to make more sustainable choices. The company's "Worn Wear" program offers customers the opportunity to trade in their used Patagonia gear for store credit, which can be used toward the purchase of new or used items. The brand also supports grassroots environmental initiatives through its "1% for the Planet" program, where it donates 1% of its annual sales to support environmental causes.

FabIndia: FabIndia is an Indian brand that specializes in producing and selling ethnic wear, home furnishings, and organic products made from traditional techniques, skills, and hand-based processes. Founded in 1960, the brand has consistently prioritized sustainability and ethical practices in its business operations. FabIndia sources its materials from rural artisans and craftsmen across the country, ensuring that traditional skills and techniques are preserved and passed down through generations. By providing a platform for these artisans, FabIndia promotes sustainable livelihoods and contributes to the economic development of rural communities. The brand also emphasizes the use of natural, eco-friendly materials in its products and is committed to minimizing its environmental footprint.

ITC Limited: ITC Limited is a diversified conglomerate with interests in sectors such as FMCG, hotels, paperboards, and packaging. The company has been a pioneer in integrating sustainability into its business operations. It has set ambitious goals to become water and carbon positive and achieve zero waste to landfill. ITC's "Well-being Out of Waste" (WOW) initiative focuses on promoting recycling and waste management practices among households, commercial establishments, and educational institutions. The program has reached millions of citizens across India and has led to the collecting and recycling of thousands of tons of waste. In addition, ITC's hotel's division, ITC Hotels, has adopted a "Responsible Luxury" ethos, incorporating eco-friendly practices such as energy and water conservation, waste management, and the use of local and sustainable materials in its properties.

Tata Motors: Tata Motors, one of India's leading automobile manufacturers, has made significant strides in adopting sustainable and ethical practices in its operations. The company has implemented various measures to reduce its environmental impact, such as water conservation, energy efficiency, and waste reduction initiatives across its manufacturing facilities. Tata Motors is also committed to developing eco-friendly vehicles, with its range of electric vehicles (EVs) and hybrid vehicles leading the way in India's push toward sustainable mobility. The company's EV offerings, such as the Tata Nexon EV and the Tata Tigor EV, have gained popularity among Indian consumers for their performance, affordability, and low environmental impact.

These case studies showcase the growing trend of businesses in India embracing sustainability and ethical practices in their operations. By prioritizing long-term success over short-term gains and focusing on positively impacting society and the environment, these brands have set a strong example for others to follow.

10

Navigating the Regulatory Environment

Understanding India's Regulatory Framework

India's regulatory framework is a complex and dynamic system of rules, regulations, and guidelines that govern various aspects of businesses operating in the country. The regulatory environment in India has undergone significant changes over the years, with the government working towards creating a more business-friendly environment. However, navigating this framework can be a daunting task for businesses, especially for those new to the Indian market. This sub-chapter aims to provide an overview of the key aspects of India's regulatory framework that businesses should be aware of.

The Constitution and the Legal System India follows a federal structure of governance, with powers divided between the central government and the states. The Constitution of India is the supreme law of the land, and all other laws and regulations must conform to its provisions. India's legal system is based on a combination of common law and statutory law, with the judiciary playing a crucial role in interpreting and enforcing the laws.

Business Regulations There are numerous laws and regulations that govern businesses in India, including the Companies Act, the Income Tax Act, the Goods and Services Tax (GST) Act, and various labor laws. Some of the key aspects of these regulations include Company Formation and Registration: Businesses need to register with the Ministry of Corporate Affairs (MCA) and comply with the provisions of the Companies Act, which governs matters such as company formation, management, and dissolution. Taxation: India has a comprehensive taxation regime, with direct and indirect taxes on businesses. The Income Tax Act governs direct taxes, such as corporate income tax and personal income tax, while the GST Act governs indirect taxes levied on the supply of goods and services. Labor Laws: Businesses in India need to comply with a range of labor laws, which govern areas such as wages, working hours, employee benefits, and dispute resolution. Some of the key labor laws include the Minimum Wages Act, the Payment of Wages Act, the Industrial Disputes Act, and the Employees' Provident Fund Act.

Sector-specific Regulations In addition to the general business regulations, there are several sector-specific regulations that businesses need to be aware of, depending on the nature of their operations. Some examples include Foreign Direct Investment (FDI) Policy: India has a sector-specific FDI policy that governs the extent and conditions under which foreign investments can be made in various sectors. Businesses need to ensure compliance with the

FDI policy and the regulations of the Reserve Bank of India (RBI), the central bank and regulator for foreign exchange transactions. Telecommunications: The Department of Telecommunications (DoT) is the primary regulatory body for the telecommunications sector in India, and businesses in this sector need to comply with the guidelines and licensing requirements laid down by the DoT. Pharmaceuticals and Medical Devices: The Central Drugs Standard Control Organization (CDSCO) is responsible for regulating the pharmaceutical and medical device industries in India. Companies in these sectors must comply with the relevant provisions of the Drugs and Cosmetics Act and the Medical Device Rules.

Various laws, including the Patents Act, the Copyright Act, the Trademarks Act, and the Designs Act govern Intellectual Property (IP) Protection India's IP regime. Businesses must ensure that their IP assets are adequately protected and comply with the relevant IP laws and regulations.

Environmental Regulations Businesses in India need to comply with various environmental regulations, which govern pollution control, waste management, and natural resource conservation. Key environmental laws include the Environment (Protection) Act, the Water (Prevention and Control of Pollution) Act, and the Air (Prevention and Control of Pollution) Act. In addition to these central laws, there may also be state-specific environmental regulations that businesses need to be aware of.

Consumer Protection Consumer protection is an important aspect of India's regulatory framework, with several laws in place to safeguard the interests of consumers. The Consumer Protection Act is the primary legislation governing consumer rights, and it establishes a three-tier consumer dispute redressal mechanism at the district, state, and national levels. Businesses must ensure that their products and services meet the required quality and safety standards and that they adhere to fair trade practices.

E-commerce Regulations With the rapid growth of e-commerce in India, the government has introduced various regulations to govern this sector. The Information Technology (IT) Act and the Intermediary Guidelines Rules govern aspects such as data protection, privacy, and intermediary liability. E-commerce businesses also need to comply with the FDI policy for the e-commerce sector, which lays down certain restrictions and conditions for foreign investments in this space.

Compliance and Enforcement Ensuring compliance with India's regulatory framework is crucial for businesses operating in the country. Non-compliance can lead to various penalties, including fines, imprisonment, and even the cancellation of licenses and permits. Various authorities, such as the MCA, the Income Tax Department, the GST Council, and the respective sector-specific regulators carry out the enforcement of regulations.

Navigating India's regulatory environment can be challenging, especially for businesses new to the market or expanding their operations. It is crucial for businesses to have a thorough understanding of the relevant laws and regulations and to seek expert guidance to ensure compliance and avoid potential pitfalls. By doing so, businesses can unlock the immense potential of the Indian market while minimizing risks and ensuring sustainable growth.

Compliance and Legal Considerations for Businesses in India

1. Operating a business in India requires navigating a complex regulatory landscape. Companies must adhere to a wide range of legal requirements, spanning from corporate governance to taxation and labor laws. This sub-chapter will provide an overview of key compliance and legal considerations that businesses in India must address.

2. Company Formation and Corporate Governance, The first step in establishing a business in India is choosing the appropriate legal structure. Options include sole proprietorships, limited liability partnerships (LLPs), private limited companies, and public limited companies. Each structure has its own set of compliance requirements and tax implications. For example, private limited companies must comply with the Companies Act 2013, which governs aspects such as company registration, board meetings, and annual filings with the Ministry of Corporate Affairs (MCA).

3. Taxation Businesses in India are subject to various taxes, including corporate income tax, goods and services tax (GST), customs duties, and other indirect taxes. Companies must ensure timely filing of tax returns and payment of taxes to avoid penalties. Proper tax planning and understanding of tax incentives and exemptions can help businesses minimize their tax liabilities.

4. Labor Laws India has numerous labor laws regulating aspects such as minimum wages, working hours, employee benefits, and safety standards. The government has recently consolidated

several labor laws into four codes - the Code on Wages, the Code on Social Security, the Code on Industrial Relations, and the Code on Occupational Safety, Health, and Working Conditions. Businesses must comply with these codes and any other applicable labor laws to avoid legal disputes and maintain a positive work environment.

5. Intellectual Property Rights Protecting intellectual property (IP) is crucial for businesses, providing a competitive advantage and ensuring long-term growth. India has a well-developed IP regime covering patents, trademarks, copyrights, and designs. Companies should identify their IP assets and take appropriate steps to register and protect them. They should also be aware of potential IP infringements and have strategies in place to address them.

6. Data Protection and Privacy With the increasing importance of data in today's digital economy, businesses must ensure the protection of personal and sensitive data. India's primary legislation on data protection is the Information Technology (IT) Act 2000 and the IT (Reasonable Security Practices and Procedures and Sensitive Personal Data or Information) Rules 2011. The government is also in the process of introducing a comprehensive data protection law - the Personal Data Protection (PDP) Bill. Companies must be aware of their obligations under these laws and implement necessary safeguards to protect data.

7. Environmental Regulations Companies in India must adhere to various environmental laws, such as the Environment (Protection) Act, the Water (Prevention and Control of Pollution) Act, and the Air (Prevention and Control of Pollution) Act. These laws

regulate aspects such as pollution control, waste management, and environmental clearances. Non-compliance can result in penalties and damage to the company's reputation.

8. Anti-Corruption and Bribery Laws India has strict anti-corruption laws, including the Prevention of Corruption Act, which governs corruption in the public sector, and the Companies Act 2013, which addresses corporate fraud and corruption. Companies must establish internal controls and procedures to prevent corruption and ensure compliance with these laws.

9. Dispute Resolution Business disputes in India can be resolved through litigation, arbitration, mediation, or conciliation. Understanding the pros and cons of each method can help businesses choose the most suitable option for their specific situation. Companies should also have a robust legal strategy in place to manage disputes and minimize potential risks.

10. Competition Law Competition laws in India are governed by the Competition Act of 2002, which aims to prevent practices that have an adverse effect on competition and protect consumer interests. The Competition Commission of India (CCI) is responsible for enforcing the Act. Businesses must ensure that their practices, such as pricing, marketing, and collaborations, comply with competition laws and do not engage in anti-competitive behavior.

11. Foreign Investment Regulations India has liberalized its foreign investment policies over the years, allowing foreign direct investment (FDI) in most sectors under the automatic route.

However, some sectors have specific restrictions and caps on FDI and compliance requirements under the Foreign Exchange Management Act (FEMA) and other regulations. Companies receiving foreign investment or investing in India must ensure compliance with these regulations and obtain necessary approvals from relevant authorities.

12. Import and Export Regulations Businesses involved in international trade must comply with India's import and export regulations, including obtaining necessary licenses, adhering to customs procedures, and paying applicable duties and taxes. Companies must also be aware of any trade restrictions, such as embargoes and sanctions, and comply with the World Trade Organization (WTO) requirements and other international trade agreements to which India is a party.

13. Industry-specific Regulations Certain industries in India are subject to additional regulations and licensing requirements, such as telecommunications, pharmaceuticals, food and beverages, and financial services. Companies operating in these sectors must comply with the specific regulatory requirements and obtain necessary licenses and approvals from relevant authorities.

14. Corporate Social Responsibility (CSR) Under the Companies Act 2013, certain companies are required to spend at least 2% of their average net profits on CSR activities. Eligible companies must have a CSR policy and a CSR committee and report on their CSR initiatives in their annual reports. CSR activities can

include initiatives related to education, health, environmental sustainability, and rural development, among others.

In conclusion, businesses operating in India must be aware of the various compliance and legal considerations and take proactive steps to address them. Engaging competent legal counsel and compliance professionals can help companies navigate the complex regulatory environment, ensure compliance with applicable laws, and minimize potential risks. Staying up-to-date with regulatory changes and developments is also crucial, as it allows businesses to adapt their operations and strategies accordingly.

In summary, navigating India's regulatory landscape can be challenging, but a thorough understanding of compliance and legal requirements is essential for businesses to succeed and minimize risks. By staying informed of regulatory developments and engaging the right professionals, companies can effectively manage their legal and compliance obligations, fostering sustainable growth and success in the Indian market.

Strategies for Minimizing Risks and Maximizing Opportunities in the Indian Market

Conduct Thorough Market Research

Understanding the nuances of the Indian market is crucial for minimizing risks and maximizing opportunities. Conduct thorough market research to identify target demographics, analyze consumer behavior, understand regional differences, and assess the competition. This information will help you make informed decisions about product and service offerings, pricing strategies, distribution channels, and marketing approaches.

Localize Your Offering

India is a diverse country with varying tastes, preferences, and cultural practices. Adapting your products and services to cater to local preferences can significantly impact your success. Localization may involve customizing your offerings, packaging, or even communication strategies to resonate with local consumers. This approach can help you gain a competitive edge and foster customer loyalty.

Build a Robust Legal and Compliance Framework

A strong legal and compliance framework can help your business mitigate risks associated with India's regulatory environment. Engage competent legal counsel and compliance professionals to ensure your operations comply with all applicable laws and regulations. They can also help you stay up-to-date with regulatory changes, allowing you to adapt your strategies accordingly.

Develop a Risk Management Strategy

A well-defined risk management strategy can help your business identify, assess, and mitigate potential risks. This may include conducting regular risk assessments, implementing risk mitigation measures, and continuously monitoring and reviewing risks to address them proactively. A robust risk management strategy can minimize the impact of unforeseen events on your business.

Invest in Technology and Innovation

Embracing technological advancements and innovation can help your business stay ahead of the curve in the rapidly evolving Indian market. Invest in digital marketing, e-commerce platforms, and data analytics to better understand your customers and improve your marketing efforts. Integrating technology into your operations can also enhance efficiency, reduce costs, and improve overall business performance.

Build Strong Partnerships and Collaborations

Establishing strong partnerships and collaborations with local players can help your business access valuable resources, knowledge, and networks. Collaborations can also help you share risks, reduce costs, and increase your market presence. Choose your partners carefully, considering factors such as their reputation, expertise, and alignment with your business goals.

1. Focus on Sustainability and Ethical Practices

Adopting sustainable and ethical practices can help your business attract socially conscious consumers and enhance your brand image. This may include implementing environmentally friendly production processes, engaging in fair labor practices, or adopting transparent supply chain management. Incorporating sustainability into your business operations and marketing strategies can set you apart from competitors and contribute to long-term success.

2. Embrace Cultural and Demographic Diversity

India's diverse population offers many business opportunities that can effectively cater to different cultural and demographic segments.

Develop inclusive marketing campaigns that resonate with various consumer groups and showcase your commitment to embracing diversity. This approach can help your business tap into new markets and appeal to a broader customer base.

3. Stay Agile and Adapt to Market Changes

The Indian market is constantly evolving, and businesses must stay agile to remain competitive. Monitor market trends, consumer preferences, and regulatory developments closely, and be prepared to adapt your strategies accordingly. Embracing change and adapting to market dynamics can help your business minimize risks and capitalize on emerging opportunities.

4. Invest in Human Capital

Attracting and retaining talented employees is essential for the success of your business in the Indian market. Invest in employee training and development programs to build a skilled and motivated workforce. Cultivate a positive work environment and offer competitive compensation packages to retain top talent.

5. Leverage Government Incentives and Programs

The Indian government offers various incentives and programs to attract foreign investments and promote domestic businesses. These incentives may include tax holidays, subsidies, and simplified regulations. Stay informed about such government schemes and evaluate their applicability to your business. Leveraging these incentives can help your business reduce costs and improve your competitive position in the market.

6. Maintain Strong Customer Relationships

Building and maintaining strong relationships with your customers is crucial for long-term success in the Indian market. Implement effective customer relationship management (CRM) strategies to ensure consistent communication, gather feedback, and address customer concerns. Focus on providing excellent customer service to create loyal customers and generate positive word-of-mouth referrals.

7. Establish a Strong Brand Presence

Developing a strong brand presence is essential for standing out in the crowded Indian market. Create a compelling brand story that resonates with your target audience and communicates your unique value proposition. Implement a consistent branding strategy across all touchpoints, including your product packaging, advertising campaigns, and digital platforms. A strong brand presence can help your business differentiate itself from competitors and create a loyal customer base.

8. Diversify Your Offerings

Diversifying your product or service offerings can help your business mitigate risks associated with market fluctuations and changing consumer preferences. Offering a diverse range of products and services can also help you cater to different consumer segments and expand your market reach. Regularly review and update your product portfolio to stay relevant in the ever-evolving Indian market.

9. Monitor Your Competition

Keeping a close eye on your competitors is essential for staying ahead in the Indian market. Regularly monitor your competitors' strategies, product offerings, pricing, and marketing efforts to identify potential gaps and opportunities. Use this information to refine your strategies, stay competitive, and capitalize on market opportunities.

In conclusion, minimizing risks and maximizing opportunities in the Indian market requires a combination of research, localization, compliance, risk management, innovation, partnerships, sustainability, adaptability, talent management, leveraging government incentives, building customer relationships, establishing a strong brand presence, diversifying offerings, and monitoring the competition. By incorporating these strategies, companies can navigate the challenges and complexities of the Indian market and set themselves up for long-term success.

In summary, businesses that want to succeed in the Indian market must adopt a multi-faceted approach that includes thorough research, localization, strong legal and compliance frameworks, risk management, technology integration, strategic partnerships, sustainability, cultural sensitivity, agility, talent management, leveraging government incentives, building customer relationships, establishing a strong brand presence, diversifying offerings, and monitoring the competition. By implementing these strategies, companies can minimize risks and maximize opportunities in the dynamic and challenging Indian market.

11

Fostering Innovation and Entrepreneurship

Encouraging a Culture of Innovation within Organizations

Introduction

Innovation and entrepreneurship are the driving forces behind the growth and success of any organization. Encouraging a culture of innovation within organizations not only helps in staying competitive but also in adapting to the ever-changing business environment. This subchapter will explore the various ways organizations can foster a culture of innovation and encourage employees to think creatively and entrepreneurially.

1. Leadership and Vision

Leaders play a pivotal role in fostering a culture of innovation. The leadership team should have a clear vision of the organization's future and communicate this vision to employees effectively. When employees understand the organization's goals, they are more likely to develop innovative ideas that align with them. Moreover, leaders should lead by example, take risks, and embrace change to inspire employees to do the same.

2. Encourage Open Communication

Open communication is a critical factor in fostering innovation. Organizations should create an environment where employees feel comfortable sharing their ideas, opinions, and concerns without the fear of being judged or criticized. Encourage employees to express their thoughts and provide them with platforms such as suggestion boxes, brainstorming sessions, and open-door policies to facilitate open communication.

3. Empower Employees

Empower your employees by giving them the autonomy and responsibility to make decisions and take risks. Encourage them to experiment and learn from their failures without penalizing them for mistakes. Empowered employees are more likely to be creative, motivated, and committed to the organization's success.

4. Provide Resources and Support

Innovation requires resources and support. Organizations should provide employees with access to the necessary tools, technologies, and training to help them develop their skills and ideas. Additionally, provide financial support for innovative projects and invest in research and development to encourage a culture of innovation.

5. Foster Collaboration

Encourage employees to collaborate and share ideas across teams and departments. Cross-functional collaboration can lead to innovative ideas and solutions, as employees can bring different perspectives, skills, and experiences to the table. Use team-building exercises, workshops, and collaborative tools to facilitate teamwork and cooperation.

6. Recognize and Reward Innovation

Recognizing and rewarding innovation is crucial in creating an innovative culture. Acknowledge employees' innovative ideas and efforts through various means, such as monetary rewards, promotions, recognition programs, or public appreciation. Employees who feel valued for their contributions are more likely to continue generating innovative ideas.

7. Encourage Continuous Learning

Continuous learning is an essential aspect of fostering innovation. Encourage employees to expand their knowledge and skills through training programs, workshops, seminars, and conferences. Support their professional development by providing access to online courses, industry publications, and other learning resources. A learning culture promotes innovation by inspiring employees to think outside the box and explore new ideas.

8. Create a Safe Environment for Failure

Innovation involves taking risks, and failure is an inevitable part of the process. Organizations should create a safe environment for employees to fail without fear of consequences. Encourage employees to learn from their failures and use the lessons to improve their ideas and solutions. Embracing failure as an essential component of innovation can drive a culture of creativity and experimentation.

9. Set Clear Expectations and Metrics

Clearly define the expectations and metrics for innovation in your organization. Establish goals and key performance indicators (KPIs) that reflect the organization's commitment to innovation. This will help employees understand what is expected of them and allow them to track their progress toward achieving these goals.

10. Encourage External Partnerships

Organizations should not limit themselves to internal resources and ideas. Collaborate with external partners, such as universities, research institutes, and startups, to gain access to new perspectives and ideas. External partnerships can also provide valuable insights into emerging trends and technologies that can drive innovation within the organization.

Fostering an organization's innovation culture requires a multifaceted approach that includes strong leadership, open communication, employee empowerment, resource provision, collaboration, recognition, continuous learning, embracing failure, clear expectations, and external partnerships. By adopting these strategies, organizations can create an environment that encourages employees to think creatively and entrepreneurially, leading to sustained growth and success in an increasingly competitive business landscape.

By incorporating these strategies, companies can expect to see increased employee engagement, improved problem-solving, and more innovative ideas and solutions being generated. As a result, organizations that embrace a culture of innovation will be better equipped to adapt to changes in the market and stay ahead of the competition. Ultimately, fostering innovation and entrepreneurship within an organization is essential for long-term growth and success in today's fast-paced, ever-evolving business world.

Encouraging a Culture of Innovation within Organizations in India

Introduction

India has emerged as a hub for innovation and entrepreneurship, driven by the rapid growth of its technology sector and an increasingly skilled workforce. To stay competitive and capitalize on this momentum, organizations in India must foster a culture of innovation. In this chapter, we will explore 11 key strategies to encourage innovation within organizations and provide practical examples tailored to the Indian context.

Leadership and Vision

A strong vision and leadership are essential for cultivating a culture of innovation. Organizational leaders should establish a clear vision for innovation, emphasizing its importance for the company's long-term success. Leaders can communicate this vision through company-wide meetings, internal communications, and performance reviews. They should also set an example by actively participating in innovation initiatives and embracing new ideas.

Example: Tata Group, one of India's largest conglomerates, has long emphasized the importance of innovation. Its leaders consistently encourage innovation through various initiatives, such as the Tata Innovista competition, which celebrates groundbreaking ideas and projects across the organization.

Encourage Open Communication

Open communication is crucial for fostering innovation, as it allows employees to share ideas, discuss challenges, and collaborate on solutions. Organizations should establish communication channels that facilitate idea sharing and feedback, such as suggestion boxes, online forums, and regular brainstorming sessions.

Example: Infosys, a leading Indian IT services company, encourages open communication through its internal social network, InfyBubble. This platform allows employees to share ideas, collaborate on projects, and engage with leaders.

Empower Employees

Empowering employees to take ownership of their work and make decisions can significantly boost innovation. Organizations can empower employees by giving them the autonomy to pursue new ideas and the resources and support needed to bring these ideas to fruition.

Example: HCL Technologies, an Indian IT services company, introduced its "Employees First, Customers Second" philosophy to empower its workforce. By giving employees the authority to make decisions and take risks, HCL has fostered a culture of innovation and achieved significant business growth.

Provide Resources and Support

To nurture innovation, organizations should provide employees with the resources and support needed to explore and develop new ideas. This can include funding, dedicated innovation teams, access to technology and tools, and opportunities to attend conferences or workshops.

Example: Mahindra & Mahindra, an Indian multinational conglomerate, established the Mahindra Innovation Academy to support its employees' innovation efforts. The academy offers training, resources, and mentoring to help employees bring their ideas to life.

Foster Collaboration

Collaboration is essential for innovation, as it allows employees to combine their knowledge, skills, and perspectives to generate new ideas and solve complex problems. Organizations can foster collaboration by encouraging cross-functional teamwork, holding collaborative workshops and events, and investing in collaborative tools and technologies.

Example: Wipro, a leading Indian IT services company, launched its Topcoder platform to promote collaboration and crowdsourced innovation. The platform connects Wipro employees with a global community of developers, designers, and data scientists, enabling them to collaborate on innovative projects and solutions.

Recognize and Reward Innovation

Recognizing and rewarding innovation can motivate employees to think creatively and take risks. Organizations can implement recognition programs, such as innovation awards or spot bonuses, to celebrate employees' innovative achievements and contributions.

Example: Godrej, an Indian conglomerate, created the Godrej Innovation Awards to recognize employees who develop groundbreaking ideas and solutions. The awards celebrate the winners and inspire other employees to innovate.

Encourage Continuous Learning

A culture of continuous learning is essential for innovation, as it ensures that employees stay up-to-date with the latest knowledge, trends, and technologies. Organizations can encourage continuous learning by offering training programs, providing access to online learning resources, and supporting employees in pursuing further education or certifications.

Example: Reliance Industries Limited, a major Indian conglomerate, has partnered with leading educational institutions to offer its employees access to executive education programs. These programs help employees develop new skills and stay current with industry trends, fostering a culture of continuous learning and innovation.

Create a Safe Environment for Failure

Innovation involves taking risks, and not all ideas will succeed. To encourage employees to experiment and think outside the box, organizations must create an environment where failure is accepted and treated as a learning opportunity. Leaders should emphasize the importance of learning from mistakes and celebrate the efforts behind failed projects rather than focusing solely on success.

Example: Google India promotes a culture of experimentation and learning from failure through its "20% time" policy. This policy allows employees to spend 20% of their work time pursuing personal projects and ideas, even if they might not result in immediate success. This approach has led to the development of numerous innovative products and services.

Set Clear Expectations and Metrics

Setting clear expectations and metrics for innovation can help organizations measure progress and ensure that innovation efforts are aligned with business goals. Key performance indicators (KPIs), such as the number of new ideas generated, the percentage of revenue from new products, or the time taken to bring an idea to market, can provide a framework for evaluating innovation performance.

Example: ICICI Bank, one of India's largest private banks, has established clear innovation KPIs to track the success of its innovation initiatives. By regularly monitoring and reporting on these KPIs, the bank ensures that its innovation efforts contribute to its overall business objectives.

Encourage External Partnerships

External partnerships can provide organizations with access to new ideas, technologies, and markets. By collaborating with startups, research institutions, or other companies, organizations can tap into external sources of innovation and drive growth.

Example: Marico, an Indian consumer goods company, established the Marico Innovation Foundation (MIF) to collaborate with external partners on innovative projects. The MIF has partnered with startups, academic institutions, and industry experts to develop new products, services, and business models that have contributed to Marico's growth and success.

Conclusion

Creating a culture of innovation is critical for organizations in India to stay competitive and capitalize on the country's rapid growth and development. By implementing the strategies outlined in this chapter, such as establishing strong leadership and vision, encouraging open communication, empowering employees, providing resources and support, fostering collaboration, recognizing and rewarding innovation, promoting continuous learning, creating a safe environment for failure, setting clear expectations and metrics, and encouraging external partnerships, organizations can unlock the full potential of their employees and drive long-term success.

Future Trends and Opportunities for Indian Entrepreneurs

As the Indian economy continues to evolve and adapt to the rapidly changing global landscape, numerous opportunities are emerging for entrepreneurs in various sectors. Here are some of the key trends and opportunities that Indian entrepreneurs can leverage to drive growth and success in the coming years.

Artificial Intelligence (AI) and Machine Learning (ML) AI and ML have the potential to revolutionize the way businesses operate, and entrepreneurs can benefit immensely from incorporating these technologies into their ventures. Some of the potential applications include:

- Automating repetitive tasks allows entrepreneurs to focus on more strategic aspects of their businesses.

- Enhancing customer service through AI-powered chatbots and virtual assistants.

- Improving decision-making by analyzing vast amounts of data and deriving actionable insights.

- Streamlining supply chain management and optimizing inventory levels through advanced demand forecasting techniques.

By integrating AI and ML into their businesses, entrepreneurs can improve efficiency, reduce costs, and gain a competitive edge in the market.

The Metaverse The metaverse is a virtual, interconnected universe that combines aspects of social media, gaming, and augmented reality. As this concept gains traction, entrepreneurs can explore various opportunities to create unique products, services, and experiences within the metaverse. These can include:

- Developing virtual real estate and digital assets.

- Creating immersive brand experiences and marketing campaigns within virtual environments.

- Building virtual communities and platforms for networking, collaboration, and entertainment.

- Offering virtual goods and services, such as fashion, art, and educational content.

Blockchain Technology Blockchain, the decentralized and secure digital ledger technology behind cryptocurrencies, offers numerous applications for entrepreneurs across various industries. Some potential use cases include:

- Implementing smart contracts for more efficient and transparent business transactions.

- Enhancing supply chain traceability and transparency.

- Developing decentralized applications (dApps) that offer increased user security and privacy.

- Establishing decentralized finance (DeFi) platforms to provide alternative financial services to underserved populations.

By leveraging blockchain technology, entrepreneurs can build innovative solutions that address existing challenges and inefficiencies in traditional systems.

FinTech Advancements Financial technology (FinTech) continues to disrupt the financial services industry, offering new opportunities for entrepreneurs to develop innovative products and services. Some areas of potential growth in FinTech include:

- Digital payments and remittances make transactions faster, cheaper, and more secure.

- Peer-to-peer (P2P) lending platforms connect borrowers with investors, bypassing traditional financial institutions.

- InsurTech solutions that leverage AI and ML to offer personalized insurance products and improve risk assessment.

- Robo-advisory platforms that use algorithms to offer automated financial planning and investment advice.

By tapping into the FinTech revolution, entrepreneurs can create new business models that cater to the evolving needs of consumers and businesses.

Sustainable and Eco-friendly Solutions As environmental concerns gain prominence; there is a growing demand for sustainable and eco-friendly products and services. Entrepreneurs can capitalize on this trend by:

- Developing innovative solutions that minimize waste, reduce energy consumption, and promote the circular economy.

- Creating eco-friendly alternatives to traditional products, such as biodegradable packaging, plant-based foods, and renewable energy sources.

- Offering services that help consumers and businesses adopt sustainable practices, such as energy audits, waste management, and carbon offset programs.

By embracing sustainability, entrepreneurs can positively impact the environment while catering to the increasing consumer demand for eco-friendly solutions.

HealthTech and Wellness The COVID-19 pandemic has highlighted the importance of health and wellness, creating numerous opportunities for entrepreneurs in this sector. Some potential areas for growth include:

- Telemedicine platforms that facilitate remote consultations and medical services.

- Wearable devices and apps that track and monitor health metrics, such as sleep, nutrition, and activity levels.

- Mental health and wellness apps that offer support, resources, and personalized interventions to users.

- Innovative solutions that enable personalized medicine, such as genomics, AI-powered diagnostics, and targeted therapies.

By tapping into the health and wellness market, entrepreneurs can address the growing demand for accessible and personalized healthcare solutions.

EdTech and E-Learning Education technology (EdTech) and e-learning have witnessed tremendous growth, with more people seeking online and digital learning solutions. Entrepreneurs can explore numerous opportunities in this sector, such as:

- Online learning platforms that offer courses, certifications, and degrees from renowned institutions.

- Adaptive learning solutions that leverage AI and ML to deliver personalized learning experiences.

- Virtual and augmented reality-based learning tools that create immersive educational experiences.

- Collaboration and communication tools that enable remote learning and facilitate interaction between students, teachers, and peers.

By investing in EdTech and e-learning, entrepreneurs can transform the education landscape and make quality education accessible to a wider audience.

Gig Economy and Remote Work gig and remote work have gained prominence, with more people opting for flexible and freelance work arrangements. Entrepreneurs can capitalize on this trend by developing platforms and solutions that cater to the needs of gig workers and remote employees, such as:

- Freelance marketplaces that connect professionals with clients seeking their skills and expertise.

- Project management and collaboration tools that facilitate remote teamwork and communication.

- Co-working spaces and virtual offices that provide a conducive work environment for remote workers.

- Training and upskilling platforms that help gig workers and remote employees stay competitive in the job market.

By focusing on the gig economy and remote work, entrepreneurs can create innovative solutions that cater to the evolving world of work.

In conclusion, the future holds immense potential for Indian entrepreneurs, with numerous trends and opportunities shaping the business landscape. By embracing these trends and capitalizing on emerging opportunities, entrepreneurs can create innovative solutions that address the changing needs of consumers and businesses while driving growth and success in the rapidly evolving Indian market.

12

Conclusion

Key Takeaways from the Book

As we reach the conclusion of this book, it's important to reflect on the key takeaways that will help you navigate the ever-changing Indian market successfully. You can adapt and thrive in this dynamic environment by understanding the market landscape, embracing innovation, leveraging digital and social media, and staying informed about emerging trends.

1. Embrace Innovation: A core theme of this book is the importance of innovation in the modern business landscape. Whether you're a startup or an established organization, continuously seeking to innovate and improve your products, services, and operations is crucial to staying competitive and relevant.

2. Understand the Indian Market: Recognizing the unique characteristics of the Indian market, including its cultural, demographic, and economic diversity, will help you tailor your

offerings and marketing strategies to resonate with your target audience effectively.

3. Leverage Social Media and Digital Marketing: Harnessing the power of social media and digital marketing channels is essential for reaching and engaging with your audience. Stay up-to-date with the latest platforms and trends, and be prepared to adapt your strategies as needed.

4. Focus on Sustainability and Ethical Practices: Businesses that prioritize sustainability and ethical practices will not only appeal to an increasingly conscious consumer base but will also contribute to a healthier environment and society. Integrating these principles into your business operations and marketing strategies is essential for long-term success.

5. Navigate the Regulatory Environment: Familiarize yourself with the regulatory framework governing your industry and ensure that your business complies with all relevant laws and regulations. By staying informed and proactive, you can minimize risks and maximize opportunities.

6. Foster Innovation and Entrepreneurship: Encourage a culture of innovation within your organization and support the growth of the entrepreneurial ecosystem in India. Collaborating with others, sharing ideas, and embracing new technologies can help drive progress and success in the market.

7. Stay Informed about Future Trends: Keep an eye on emerging trends and opportunities, such as AI, blockchain, the metaverse, and advances in fintech. By staying informed and open to new

ideas, you can position your business to capitalize on these developments and stay ahead of the competition.

In conclusion, navigating the complexities of the Indian market requires a combination of adaptability, innovation, and a deep understanding of the diverse landscape. By incorporating the insights and strategies shared in this book, you will be well-equipped to succeed and grow in this dynamic market. Remember that the key to success lies in your ability to learn, adapt, and evolve alongside the ever-changing landscape of the Indian market. Embrace the challenges and opportunities that lie ahead, and you will be on the path to creating a successful, innovative, and sustainable business in India.

The Importance of Continuous Innovation in India's Evolving Market

India's rapidly evolving market presents both challenges and opportunities for businesses operating within its borders. The country's dynamic economy, diverse population, and growing middle class demand that businesses be agile and responsive to market shifts. One of the key drivers of success in this context is continuous innovation, which allows organizations to stay ahead of the curve and remain competitive.

1. Meeting Consumer Needs and Preferences The diverse nature of the Indian market means that businesses must be adaptable in catering to their target audience's varied preferences and needs. Continuous innovation enables companies to develop and refine their products and services, ensuring they remain appealing and

relevant to their customers. For example, in the food industry, businesses must cater to a range of dietary preferences, such as vegetarian, non-vegetarian, and vegan options, as well as address regional taste preferences. By constantly innovating and offering a variety of choices, businesses can keep up with the evolving demands of consumers and maintain their market share.

2. Staying Competitive in a Rapidly Changing Market Innovation is crucial for staying competitive in India's dynamic market, where new players and disruptive technologies are continually emerging. Companies that fail to innovate risk being overtaken by more agile competitors or rendered obsolete by technological advancements. Businesses must therefore invest in research and development, be open to new ideas and technologies, and foster a culture of innovation within their organizations. This will enable them to identify new opportunities, develop innovative products and services, and respond quickly to changes in the market landscape.

3. Adapting to Technological Advancements Technological advancements, such as artificial intelligence (AI), blockchain, and the Internet of Things (IoT), are rapidly transforming industries across the globe, and India is no exception. By embracing and integrating these technologies into their operations, businesses can streamline processes, reduce costs, and improve the overall customer experience. For example, AI-powered chatbots can help organizations provide 24/7 customer support, while IoT devices can enhance supply chain efficiency and enable real-time tracking of goods. Continuous innovation is essential for

businesses to adapt to these technological advancements and remain competitive in the market.

4. Enhancing Sustainability and Social Responsibility As consumers become more conscious of environmental and social issues, businesses must prioritize sustainability and ethical practices. By continuously innovating and incorporating sustainable materials, production processes, and business practices, organizations can meet consumer expectations and contribute to the well-being of society and the environment. For instance, companies can adopt circular economy principles, such as designing products for durability, using recycled materials, or offering repair services, to minimize waste and extend product lifecycles. Embracing renewable energy sources and reducing emissions are other ways businesses can innovate to become more sustainable and responsible.

5. Navigating Regulatory and Compliance Challenges India's regulatory environment is complex and constantly evolving, posing challenges for businesses operating in the country. Staying compliant with changing laws and regulations requires continuous innovation and adaptability. Companies must invest in systems and processes that enable them to remain compliant, such as automating data collection and reporting or employing legal and compliance professionals. By adopting a proactive and innovative approach to regulatory compliance, businesses can minimize risks and capitalize on opportunities in the market.

In conclusion, continuous innovation is critical for success in India's evolving market. By investing in research and development, embracing new technologies, and fostering a culture of innovation within their organizations, businesses can meet the diverse needs of consumers, stay competitive in a rapidly changing landscape, and contribute to the greater good of society and the environment. By prioritizing continuous innovation, companies can seize opportunities, overcome challenges, and thrive in India's dynamic market.

A Call to Action for Entrepreneurs and Business Leaders

The rapid growth and evolution of India's market present a plethora of opportunities for entrepreneurs and business leaders. However, to capitalize on these opportunities and navigate the challenges posed by the country's dynamic landscape, it is crucial for entrepreneurs and business leaders to take proactive steps and adopt innovative approaches. This call to action is a rallying cry for these individuals to embrace change, foster a culture of innovation, and drive sustainable growth for their organizations and the Indian economy as a whole.

1. Embrace Change and Adaptability Its diversity and constant change characterizes the Indian market. As such, entrepreneurs and business leaders must be adaptable and responsive to shifting market dynamics. This includes being open to new ideas, technologies, and business models and embracing change within their organizations. By fostering a mindset of adaptability and resilience, business leaders can better navigate the complexities of the Indian market and capitalize on emerging opportunities.

2. Foster a Culture of Innovation Innovation is the lifeblood of business success in today's rapidly evolving market.

Entrepreneurs and business leaders should actively promote innovation within their organizations by encouraging creativity, experimentation, and calculated risk-taking. This can be achieved by investing in research and development, providing employees with opportunities for skills development and growth, and recognizing and rewarding innovative ideas and solutions.

3. Prioritize Sustainability and Ethical Practices As consumer awareness of environmental and social issues grows, businesses must prioritize sustainability and ethical practices. By incorporating sustainable materials, production processes, and business practices, entrepreneurs and business leaders can meet the expectations of increasingly conscious consumers and contribute positively to society and the environment. This includes adopting circular economy principles, reducing waste, minimizing emissions, and ensuring fair labor practices across the supply chain.

4. Leverage Technology and Digital Transformation Digital transformation is a key driver of innovation and growth in today's business landscape. Entrepreneurs and business leaders must leverage the power of technology to streamline processes, enhance customer experiences, and unlock new opportunities. By adopting technologies such as artificial intelligence, machine learning, blockchain, and the Internet of Things, businesses can gain a competitive edge and drive growth in the evolving Indian market.

5. Engage with the Entrepreneurial Ecosystem India boasts a vibrant and growing entrepreneurial ecosystem, with numerous

startups, incubators, accelerators, and venture capital firms. Entrepreneurs and business leaders should actively engage with this ecosystem to access resources, support, and networking opportunities. By collaborating with other entrepreneurs, sharing knowledge, and participating in industry events, business leaders can foster innovation and growth within their organizations and the broader ecosystem.

6. Develop a Global Mindset While it is essential to understand and cater to the unique nuances of the Indian market, entrepreneurs and business leaders must also develop a global mindset. This involves being aware of global trends, embracing international best practices, and seeking opportunities for cross-border collaboration and expansion. By adopting a global outlook, businesses can tap into new markets, access valuable resources, and drive long-term growth.

7. Invest in People and Talent Development The success of any organization ultimately hinges on its people's skills, creativity, and dedication. Entrepreneurs and business leaders must invest in talent development and create a supportive and inclusive work environment that empowers employees to grow and succeed. This includes providing opportunities for continuous learning, offering competitive compensation and benefits, and fostering a diverse and inclusive culture.

In conclusion, the Indian market presents significant opportunities and challenges for entrepreneurs and business leaders. By embracing change, fostering a culture of innovation, prioritizing sustainability, leveraging technology, engaging with the entrepreneurial ecosystem, developing a global mindset, and investing in people, business leaders can seize these opportunities, overcome challenges, and drive sustainable growth for their organizations.

You Write. We Publish.

THE WRITE ORDER

To publish your own book, contact us.

We publish poetry collections, short story collections, novellas and novels.

contact@thewriteorder.com

Instagram- thewriteorder

www.facebook.com/thewriteorder

www.ingramcontent.com/pod-product-compliance
Lightning Source LLC
LaVergne TN
LVHW041910070526
838199LV00051BA/2562